Behavioural Economics

The Economy | Key Ideas

These short primers introduce students to the core concepts, theories and models, both new and established, heterodox and mainstream, contested and accepted, used by economists and political economists to understand and explain the workings of the economy.

Published

Behavioural Economics
Graham Mallard

The Living Wage
Donald Hirsch and Laura Valadez-Martinez

Behavioural Economics

Graham Mallard

agenda
publishing

For Geoff Harcourt: my role model as a compassionate economist and inspirational teacher

First published in 2017 by Agenda Publishing

Agenda Publishing Limited
The Core
Science Central
Bath Lane
Newcastle upon Tyne
NE4 5TF
www.agendapub.com

ISBN 978-1-911116-40-0 (hardcover)
ISBN 978-1-911116-41-7 (paperback)

British Library Cataloguing-in-Publication Data
A catalogue record for this book is available from the British Library

Typeset by JS Typesetting Ltd, Porthcawl, Mid Glamorgan
Printed and bound in the UK by CPI Group (UK) Ltd, Croydon, CR0 4YY

Contents

Acknowledgements

I would like to thank Hannah Wright, Beren Delbrooke-Jones, Fay Mallard and an anonymous reviewer for all their invaluable comments and suggestions about improving this book; Steven Gerrard at Agenda for his guidance; Oculi, Omni and Monnie for keeping me as sane as possible throughout the writing process; and – above all – Fay for all her love, encouragement and support, without which this would not have been possible. Thank you all.

Acknowledgement

The raison d'être of economics is the application of its principles to the explanation of the malfunctioning of the body politic and economic, and the provision of policies with which to tackle the causes of the malfunctioning.

Geoff Harcourt

1

Empiricism returns

Behavioural economics is almost certainly the most fun and influential field in economics today, setting out to explore human behaviour in all its scope and strangeness. Be it the cooperative behaviour amongst the Indonesian whale-hunters of Lamalera village or the reluctance of university students to avoid painful electrocution when presented with costless alternatives, behavioural economists seek to understand the forces that govern the decisions we make.[1] In this field lie the keys to making this world a better and more compassionate place.

The 2008 financial crash

On 15 September 2008, the fourth largest investment bank in the United States filed for the largest bankruptcy in history. For many commentators, this marked the point at which the most severe financial crash the world had experienced since 1929 became unavoidable. In the years immediately following the collapse of Lehman Brothers, some 30 million people worldwide lost their jobs due to the crash, many being consigned to long-term joblessness; poverty and inequality rates in developed countries rose to levels unprecedented in recent history, with poverty rates rising above 15 per cent in both the United States and Europe; and rates of mental illness, suicide and abuse all increased markedly. The countries hardest hit lost a decade of economic growth, but the true human costs of the crash – the devastation experienced by countless individuals and families – will never be fully understood (Okter-Robe & Podpiera 2013).

The terrible economic events of 2008–13 have led to something of a revolution within the economics discipline, for many validating the dissatisfaction amongst economics students that had been growing throughout the preceding decade. Back in June 2000, a group of university students in Paris circulated a petition calling for an increase in the realism of their economics curriculum, which they believed was too narrow, abstract and detached from the real world. The following year, 27 PhD candidates at the University of Cambridge launched their own similar petition and other students gathered at Kansas City issued a letter calling on economics departments around the world to reform their courses. In March 2003, students at Harvard University joined the fray. The "Post-Autistic Economics" movement had been born.[2]

Then came Paul Krugman's stinging criticism of the economics discipline, which suggested the reasons for this growing dissatisfaction were also the reasons for its inability to predict and prevent the financial crash. In his now infamous article in *The New York Times Magazine* on 2 September 2009, the Nobel Prize-winning economist asserted that "the central cause of the profession's failure was the desire for an all-encompassing, intellectually elegant approach that also gave economists a chance to show off their mathematical prowess." The problem, he argued, was that through being too narrowly focused on their abstract mathematics, economists had overlooked the factors that make economies vulnerable to crises: "the limitations of human rationality that often lead to bubbles and busts; to the problems of institutions that run amok; to the imperfections of markets – especially financial markets – that can cause the economy's operating system to undergo sudden, unpredictable crashes; and to the dangers created when regulators don't believe in regulation" (Krugman 2009). Krugman's view was echoed in the presentations at the inaugural conference of the Institute for New Economic Thinking in Cambridge in April 2010, which were bolstered in November 2011 when a group of Harvard undergraduates staged a walkout from their introductory macroeconomics course in support of the Occupy movement and in protest at what the organisers saw as the inequality reinforcing bias of the subject.[3]

By the time the effects of the financial crash had subsided, the pressure for economics to change – for its curricula to be more broadly conceived, more factually grounded on empirical research and less mathematically abstract – had become well established and could not be ignored. Economics began to change, with behavioural economics taking a central role.

The disagreement between friends

The nature of this conflict between the economics mainstream and its discontents is certainly not new to the twenty-first century, being at its heart about how the world can be understood. In relatively recent history, this fundamental question of epistemology – of the nature of understanding – dates back to the start of the Enlightenment movement in the mid-eighteenth century, when philosophers grappling with this issue in salons across Europe aligned themselves into two camps. On one side were the rationalists, believing that understanding comes from rational thought and logic: from exercising the human mind, which the Enlightenment had recently liberated from the binds of religious assertion and superstition. On the other side were the empiricists, arguing that understanding can only arise from experience: from observing, measuring and inspecting the real world. The two camps had the same objective, but approached it from opposing directions: the rationalists starting with our minds and using the powers of thought to create explanations to be compared to reality; the empiricists starting with reality and gathering data to be organised into explanations.

Those considering the human, rather than the natural, world – the "Worldly Philosophers" – were faced with the very same question (Heilbroner 2000). This was perhaps most evident in the disagreement between David Ricardo and Thomas Malthus: two good friends who helped to establish economics as a discipline at the turn of the nineteenth century. Ricardo (1772–1823) was a wealthy stockbroker and landowner, who is perhaps best known for his opposition to the UK Corn Laws and his demonstration of the importance of free trade: one of his many contributions to economics (or political economy as it was known at the time) that remain essential components of courses today. Ricardo was a keen rationalist who maintained that economies and the human interactions they comprise are best understood through the construction of abstract mathematical models that lead to clear and coherent predictions. Malthus (1766–1834), a graduate from Jesus College at the University of Cambridge and a cleric in the Church of England, is best known for his *Essay on the Principle of Population*. Malthus disagreed with his good friend's stance on what would come to be called economic methodology, instead asserting an empiricist position about the need to gather data from observations of the real world and using that to derive conclusions.

3

Ricardo won the debate, possibly because of his more influential position and his better-resourced supporters, which established the course the subject has navigated ever since. The fact that students today are introduced to indifference curve analysis (as shown below) in their first lectures can be traced back to the outcome of the Ricardo–Malthus methodological debate. An outcome that many later economists subsequently lamented, including Joseph Schumpeter, who coined the term "the Ricardian vice" to describe the rationalist economics approach, and John Maynard Keynes, who asserted the subject would have been better served had Malthus rather than Ricardo been its father.

The mainstream bit

Behavioural economics – and so this book – is primarily concerned with the economic decision-making of us as individuals: with the nature of our preferences, the cognitive processes we employ, the social nature of our interactions, and our susceptibility to manipulation. It is predominantly an alternative approach to mainstream microeconomics. It is helpful, then, to consider the content of most opening undergraduate microeconomics lectures before examining the alternative approach.

Consider a situation in which we are choosing what to buy with our limited finances. And for the purpose of simplicity, consider there are only two goods available, both of which are desirable. All we need do in this situation is to choose which combination – or *bundle* – of the two goods we buy. This situation is summarised in Figure 1.1. With the quantities of the two goods measured along the axes, any bundle can be represented as a point on the diagram, such as the bundles identified as A and B, comprising A_1 and A_2 and B_1 and B_2 amounts of the goods, respectively. Our fixed finances are represented by the *budget line*, which traces the bundles for which we have to spend every penny we have. The vertical and horizontal intercepts of the budget line are simply the quantities of goods 1 and 2 we can buy if we spend all we have on them, respectively, and its gradient is simply the ratio of the prices of the two goods.

Since the work of Francis Ysidro Edgeworth (1845–1926), our preferences have been represented by indifference curves, each of which traces a set of bundles between which we are indifferent. In other words, each indifference

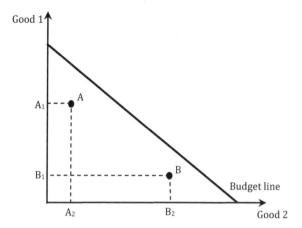

Figure 1.1 Our budget and the available bundles

curve traces a set of bundles that give us exactly the same amount of satis-faction, which economists call *utility*. Two such curves are shown in Figure 1.2. As both goods are desirable, we prefer to have more rather than less of both and so the bundles traced by IC_2 are preferred to those traced by IC_1. Indifference curves are usually curved in the convex manner shown because we tend to prefer bundles that consist of moderate quantities of both goods to bundles that consist of a large quantity of one good and only a little of the other.

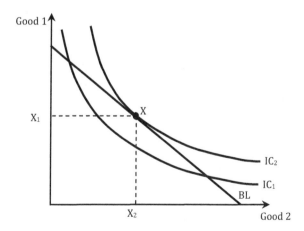

Figure 1.2 Our preferences and choice

Given our indifference curves and our budget line, we should buy the bundle on the highest indifference curve we can afford: bundle X in the diagram and so X_1 and X_2 quantities of goods 1 and 2, respectively.

John Hicks and Roy Allen presented this simple, abstract model of consumer choice in 1934 (Hicks & Allen 1934). That it continues to be a cornerstone of every introductory economics course is testament to both its usefulness and elegance, facilitating the analysis of changes in our budgets and in the prices of goods, and also of different forms of taxation. It is certainly not intended as a descriptive model of behaviour: no economist claims that we actually make consumption choices this way. Its intention is far less ambitious than that: it seeks only to represent our decision-making *as if* we are completely logical and to provide economists with a tool with which they can establish the logical effects of inevitable events.

Despite its strengths as a piece of rationalist work, it is grounded – at least implicitly – on a number of assumptions that behavioural economists have subsequently questioned:

- We employ *optimization*: that our goal when making decisions is to maximize our utility; that we seek the single option that affords us the most satisfaction possible.
- Our preferences are *complete*: that we are able to compare every possible option to one another and to rank them all according to the satisfaction they afford us.
- Our preferences are *stable*: that we maintain our ranking of options unless the nature of those options change.
- Our preferences are *reflexive*: that, when faced with two options that are absolutely identical, we are indifferent between them and so naturally assign them the same position in our ranking of options.
- Our preferences are *transitive*: that, if we prefer option A to option B, and we also prefer option B to option C, then we must logically prefer option A to option C.
- The *ownership of an item is unimportant*: that whether or not we initially possess an item does not affect our valuation of it nor our terms when it comes to trading it.
- We are *isolated* decision-makers: that we make choices based entirely on our own preferences, independently from any influence from other people; we solely seek to maximize our own utility.

Table 1.1 presents some of the work in behavioural economics that has contradicted these assumptions, all of which are examined later in the book.

Table 1.1 Violations of mainstream assumptions

Mainstream assumption	Behavioural contradiction
We employ optimization	• Bounded rationality and satisficing
Our preferences are complete	• Decision fatigue • Cognitive load
Our preferences are stable	• Hyperbolic discounting • The dual-self model
Our preferences are reflexive	• The Asian disease problem • Framing
Our preferences are transitive	• Priming
The ownership of an item is unimportant	• The endowment effect
We are isolated decision-makers	• Our other-regarding preferences • Herding and anti-herding

Behavioural economics

Behavioural economists set aside the Ricardian, rationalist approach to understanding our behaviour and adopt the Malthusian, empiricist approach instead. Starting with observations of our actual behaviour, from across the span of life, behavioural economists seek to identify universal characteristics of our behaviour and common factors that cause us to behave in different ways in different settings. Their intention is to understand and predict our behaviour without having to rely upon any untested assumptions, however logical they may be, nor the need to invoke the *as if* condition on which all rationalist work is ultimately grounded.

As an academic discipline, behavioural economics occupies the area of overlap between economics and psychology (see Figure 1.3). It does so in a very specific way, though, applying the findings and the typically more empiricist methodologies of psychology to questions and settings that have traditionally been in the remit of economics (Earl 2005). This sets it apart from the related discipline of *economic psychology*, which occupies the same academic space but works in the opposite direction, applying the findings and the typically more rationalist methodologies of economics to questions and settings that have traditionally been the concern of psychologists. The related field of *neuroeconomics* also occupies the same academic space but applies the more technological methods of neuroscience – the biological study of the human brain and nervous system – to questions and settings that have traditionally been in the remit of economics (Camerer *et al.* 2005).

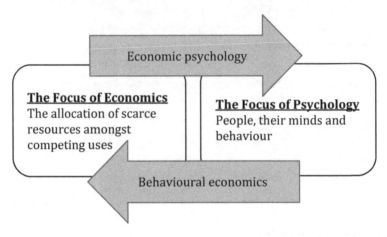

Figure 1.3 Behavioural economics and economic psychology

Methodology

Behavioural economists are primarily concerned with the collection of data through observations of our actual behaviour. There are two distinct approaches to this: *experimentation,* in which researchers collect primary data through the study of our behaviour in controlled situations, and *empirical study,* in which they take advantage of existing, often large-scale, datasets from real life situations (see Figure 1.4).

Regarding the first of these, there are four discernable types of experiments employed by behavioural economists:[4]

1. *Conventional laboratory experiments.* These consist of carefully designed artificial settings, in which the behaviour of participants (typically university students) is tightly controlled so the key effects

are easily observed. An example of this approach is the work on the *excessive choice effect*: the observation that we can be overwhelmed when faced with a large number of options and so prefer situations in which options are restricted (see Chapter 4). In the first of four experiments in one study, 48 undergraduates were asked to decide, in advance, whether they would like to choose a free soft drink from a set of six options or from a set of 24 options. 42 per cent of the participants opted for the smaller choice set: a simple experiment leading to a somewhat surprising and counter-intuitive result (Arunachalam *et al.* 2009).

2. *Artefactual field experiments.* These also consist of carefully designed and controlled artificial settings, but are conducted on non-student subjects. An investigation into how the productivity of children is affected by them first having to resist temptation is an example of such an experiment. Over 100 children of different ages at a summer camp in Padua were divided into two, roughly age-balanced, groups. Those in the temptation group were seated near a table on which there was a range of enjoyable snacks and drinks. These children were told they would soon play a game in which they could win tokens that could be traded for the treats and so they should not consume any in the meantime. The children in the control group were similarly told about the game but were not seated in close proximity to any temptation. After ten minutes, during which the two groups of children were left without any adult supervision and so during which those in the temptation group could easily sneak a treat or two, the children completed a simple origami-style task, having a further ten minutes to earn tokens for treats by folding as many sheets as possible in a stipulated manner. Children under nine years of age were found to be 21 per cent less productive when they had been subject to temptation, whereas exposure to temptation did not significantly affect those nine years or older (Bucciol *et al.* 2011). Age is clearly an important determinant of the effect of us having to resist temptation on our cognitive abilities in subsequent contexts.

3. *Framed field experiments.* These are conducted on non-student subjects but within more naturally occurring settings, either in terms of the goods, tasks or amounts of information involved. An example of such an experiment is a recent study into the effects on aid

distribution and cooperation of there being a group representative among the recipients. The researchers studied the behaviour of over 120 inhabitants of six rural villages in Nicaragua, where substantial amounts of aid had been distributed through participatory projects in the preceding years. Their experiment involved groups of eight participants each interacting over ten rounds. Each round consisted of two stages. In stage one, each participant in a group simultaneously and privately decided how much of his or her aid endowment to contribute to the group, knowing the group's collective cooperation determined the aid it attracted: greater cooperation meaning greater aid. In the second stage, the aid the group attracted was distributed among the group members. In the first five rounds, each member received the same share of the attracted aid. In the final five rounds, the participant who made the greatest contribution to the group's collective resources decided the distribution, becoming the group's representative. The results show the average contributions declined during the first five rounds but then increased during the final five: participants free-rode when the aid was equally distributed, deterring everyone from contributing; whereas when a representative distributed the aid, either the fear of punishment or the competition to become the representative drove participants to increase their contributions (D'Exelle & van der Berg 2014).

4. *Natural field experiments.* These consist of non-student subjects making very normal decisions in entirely natural situations and being completely unaware of being in a study. An example of such an experiment is an investigation into how charitable donations are affected by the advertised amount of money that has already been acquired for the cause and by the inclusion of a refund clause. The experimenters solicited donors in precisely the manner used by real charities, focusing on donors who had all recently given money to charitable causes, and invited them to make contributions to the $3,000 required for a university's environmental policy centre to purchase a much-needed computer. The study demonstrated that increasing the advertised amount already acquired from $300 to $2,010 led to a six-fold increase in donations, whilst including the refund rule – all contributions being returned if the $3,000 was not achieved – increased contributions by 20 per cent (List & Lucking-Reiley 2002).

The empirical study approach, on the other hand, involves the statistical analysis of data regarding real life behaviour in order to identify significant relationships between the decisions made in a given situation and possible explanatory variables. The household data from the German Socio-Economic Panel (GSOEP) has been analysed, for example, in an investigation of the relationship between workers' feelings of unfairness about the tax system and their rates of absenteeism from work. Respondents to the 2005 GSOEP questionnaire were asked how they perceived the tax burden of managers at the upper end of the income distribution. Excluding those who responded with "don't know", there were 4,565 respondents, of whom 72 per cent thought managers were taxed too lightly. Those who felt this way took an average of 8.78 days off work compared to the average of 5.87 days taken by those who felt managers were appropriately or excessively taxed. Once other possible explanatory factors are taken into account and controlled for, the analysis shows that a belief that the tax system is unfair – treating the highest earners too leniently – leads to a 20 per cent higher rate of absenteeism from work (Cornelissen *et al.* 2013). Perceptions about fairness lead to significant behavioural effects (see Chapter 5).

The objective of behavioural economists is to generate theories about our behaviour: stories that explain and predict how we respond in given settings, either as individuals or as members of a group. Once relevant data has been collected – either through experimentation or the statistical analysis of existing datasets – and analysed, behavioural economists use their findings

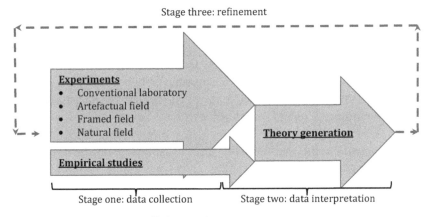

Figure 1.4 The methodology of behavioural economics

to build such theories (these are the subjects of Chapters 3–5). Once such theories are generated, they are refined through repeated testing in other settings. This is an iterative process in which understanding is developed according to Karl Popper's theory of falsification: theories lead to hypotheses, which are then tested and either proved to be false, and so discarded, or refined.

Where we go from here

It is an exciting time to embark on the study of behavioural economics. The field is expanding rapidly, with university economics departments across the world increasingly employing behavioural specialists and offering popular undergraduate behavioural modules; with new academic journals being launched to cope with – and compete with one another in – the publication of the increasingly voluminous research output; and with it even being incorporated into secondary school curricula, most notably in the new A level (16–18) specifications in the UK. The field is also becoming increasingly influential, changing the nature of modern economics as an academic discipline but also shaping the policies of governments around the globe (see Chapter 6).

Developments in behavioural economics can be categorised into the "4Ps" (Figure 1.5), which form the structure of the remainder of this book:

- *Preferences*: the common objectives that drive our behaviour (Chapter 3).
- *Processes*: the nature and effects of the actual mental procedures we commonly employ when making decisions (Chapter 4).
- *Participation*: the two-way relationship between our behaviour as individuals and the societies in which we live, the social pressures that influence us and the influence we have on our wider social groups (Chapter 5).
- *Persuasion*: the ways in which others manipulate our behaviour, for both good and ill (Chapter 6).

First of all, though, a brief evolutionary history of the field is presented in Chapter 2. The final chapter then offers an overall assessment of the field, of its successes but also its weaknesses, and a discussion of its future.

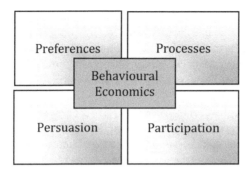

Figure 1.5 The four "Ps"

SUMMARY

- Publicly expressed dissatisfaction with the abstract and mathematical methodology of mainstream economics had been mounting for some years before the 2008 financial crash. The crash served to make this dissatisfaction impossible to ignore.
- The rationalist/empiricist debate has always been at the heart of academic pursuit and in modern economics was fought in the eighteenth century by David Ricardo and Thomas Malthus.
- The rationalist approach to scientific study has been the approach adopted by mainstream economics, leading to the development of the assumptions of rational decision-making.
- Behavioural economics brings the empirical approach back to the fore in economics.
- Four types of experiments are used in behavioural economics – conventional laboratory, artefactual field, framed field and natural field – along with empirical analysis.
- Developments in behavioural economics can be categorised into those about our preferences, cognitive processes, participatory natures and the ways we can be persuaded.

Notes

1. These examples are explored in Chapters 5 and 3, respectively.
2. See "A Brief History of the Post-Autistic Economics Movement": http://www.paecon.net/HistoryPAE.htm (accessed April 2017).

3. For views of the walkout, see *The Harvard Crimson*, 2 November 2011, "Students walk out of Ec 10 in solidarity with Occupy": http://www.thecrimson.com/article/2011/11/2/mankiw-walkout-economics-10/ and also *The New York Times* blog of Gregory Mankiw, "Know what you're protesting", http://www.nytimes.com/2011/12/04/business/know-what-youre-protesting-economic-view.html?_r=0 (accessed April 2017).

4. The taxonomy here is taken from Harrison & List (2004). They also suggest three additional types of experiment: *social* (involving the intentional manipulation of government policy), *natural* (the study of uncontrolled, naturally-occurring events) and *thought* (the use of problems to be mentally solved). Rubinstein (2007) also proposes *online* experiments, which involve the observation of participants' decisions as they respond to controlled scenarios uploaded to the Internet. For further discussion about the experimental methods used in behavioural economics, also see Charness *et al.* (2013).

2

Evolution and revolution

Since the seminal works of Daniel Kahneman and Amos Tversky in the 1970s, behavioural economics has experienced astonishing growth in both its reach and influence.[1] It is now firmly established as a field in its own right, encompassed within the wider discipline of economics (see Earl 2005):

- Three Nobel Prizes have been awarded to academics for their work relating to behavioural economics: Herbert Simon in 1978 and Daniel Kahneman and Vernon Smith in 2002.[2]
- There now exists substantially more than 50,000 papers citing the two pioneering works of Kahneman and Tversky (Burnham 2013).
- There are an ever-expanding number of dedicated academic societies (such as the Economics Science Association, the Society for the Advancement of Socio-Economics and the Society for the Advancement of Behavioural Economics) and journals (including the *Journal of Economic Behavior and Organisation*, the *Review of Behavioural Economics*, *Experimental Economics* and the *Journal of the Economics Science Association*).
- Universities are now competing with one another to offer courses in the field and the subject is being taught as part of the curriculum for A level economics in the UK.

The relationship between those studying economics as a whole and those examining economic decision-making in particular has not always been straightforward, however, and has undergone a number of shifts over the past 180 years. There is an argument that this relationship remains one of tension and distrust rather than of mutual admiration and acceptance (see Chapter 7).

The classical era

No one can be criticised for asserting that economists have always been concerned with the study of how we – as individuals, families and groups such as businesses – actually make economic decisions. With economics being commonly defined as the "science which studies human behaviour as a relationship between given ends and scarce means which have alternative uses" (Robbins 1932: 15), such an assertion seems both innocuous and self-evident.

During the era of classical economics, this assertion was certainly true. This is most clearly demonstrated in the works of Adam Smith, who is now considered the father of modern economics. Born in Scotland, kidnapped by gypsies at the age of four, educated at the University of Oxford and prone to exceptionally eccentric behaviour, Smith was actually a classical philosopher who spent most of his academic life at the University of Glasgow.[3] Writing on the eve of the industrial revolution, Smith was concerned with identifying the laws that govern human society, in a way akin to Newton's earlier interest in the laws that govern the physical world.

Smith asserted we are all endowed with moral sentiments, which ultimately drive our behaviour. In his *Theory of Moral Sentiments* (1759), Smith wrote about the absolute importance of psychological insights if we are to understand our economic actions, including those relating to habits, customs and concerns about social wealth, fairness and justice. In 1764, Smith accompanied the stepson of the then Chancellor of the Exchequer on "the grand tour" of Europe: the fashionable educational experience for children of wealthy families. Allowing him to engage with like-minded thinkers in all the major capitals of Europe, such as the Physiocrats in France, this excursion was invaluable to Smith as he organised and developed the thoughts that would form his most famous work, *The Wealth of Nations* (1776).[4] Smith later wrote that it "is not from the benevolence of the butcher, the brewer or the baker that we expect our dinner, but from their regard for their own interest"; and that by "pursuing his own interest [a person] frequently promotes that of the society more effectually than when he really intends to promote it" (Smith [1776] 1982: Bk 1, Chp 2.2 & Bk IV, Chp 2.9). His key assertion, which was truly radical, was that whenever we follow our psychological urges and strive to better our lives in a way that conforms to our moral sentiments, we inadvertently maximize the total satisfaction of society as a whole. Economic thinkers and philosophers need to understand these moral sentiments – essentially what we now call preferences (see Chapter 3) – if we are to understand the way we behave and the way the economy functions. Smith was, for many, the first behavioural economist.

Smith was certainly not the *only* behavioural economist in this early, classical era, however: indeed, the study of psychology and political economy were wholly interlinked during this period. Another was Thomas Malthus, who was a parson before arguably becoming the world's first professional economist, teaching administrators in the East India Company. Malthus is best known for two things – one methodological and the other informational – both of which are pertinent to the evolution of economics and, subsequently, to the path taken by behavioural economics. The first is for losing the debate with his best friend and fellow economic thinker, David Ricardo, over the appropriate approach to studying the economy (see Chapter 1). Ricardo favoured an abstract rationalist approach whereas Malthus argued it should be based on an examination of reality: "The tendency to premature generalization among political economists occasions also an unwillingness to bring their theories to the test of experience… A comprehensive attention to facts is necessary, both to prevent the multiplication of theories, and to confirm those which are just" (Ricardo 1820: 10–11).

The second, and perhaps strongest, reason why Malthus is remembered is for his 1798 publication, *An Essay on the Principle of Population as it Affects the Future Improvement of Society*. In this he argued that agricultural production was simply unable to expand at a rate sufficient to support the growth of the population. Malthus demonstrated that as output expanded and the incomes of workers increased, population growth also increased because of the natural urge, or preference, we have to procreate. Increased procreation would quickly erode that initial increase in income per worker and would ultimately consign the human population to periodic events of famine, disease and destitution. The economy would end up simply fluctuating around a subsistence level of income per worker in a homeostasis fashion. Hearing predictions of such seemingly irrational behaviour, at the level of both the individual and society, Thomas Carlyle called political economy the "dismal science": an epithet that has unfairly stuck.

The marginal revolution

By the 1870s, dissatisfaction with classical economic analysis was rising and there was an increasing desire amongst economic thinkers to see the discipline have greater scientific rigour, akin to the physical sciences. The consequence of this was what is now called the "marginal revolution", which arose concurrently but independently in the works of William Stanley Jevons, Carl Menger and Léon Walras, working in England, Austria and France, respectively.

The term "marginal" refers to the smallest single unit of a variable. It increasingly became the focus of economic analysis in this period because it is the key to optimization: the scientific rigour for which economic thinkers strove. For example, drinking an increasing amount of pinot noir can make our experience of a dinner much more enjoyable, particularly so depending on the nature of our company. This effect, however, is subject to *diminishing marginal utility*: the first glass leads to a greater increase in our utility than the third, which in turn leads to a greater *increase* in our utility than the fifth, and so on. However, drinking an increasing amount of wine also increases the likelihood of us feeling less than wholly well the following morning, and this effect is characterised by *increasing marginal returns*: the fifth glass of wine causes a greater increase in our expected regret than the third, which in turn causes a greater increase in our expected regret than the first. This situation is illustrated in Figure 2.1. To determine the optimal number of glasses of wine we should drink during a meal, we simply need to drink up to and including the glass for which the marginal (additional) utility is equal to the marginal (additional) expected regret: Q* in the diagram. Each of the glasses up to that labelled Q* brings us greater additional utility than additional expected regret, so it is sensible to consume these; each glass above Q* brings an additional expected regret that outweighs the additional utility, so these should be avoided.

Marginal analysis such as this, firmly established as the economists' modus operandi in Alfred Marshall's *Principles of Economics* (1890), gave the subject its scientific façade.[5] It is also both undeniably elegant and powerful, enabling economists to determine the optimal value of any variable: the optimal amount of a good that a consumer can buy, the optimal amount of profit a producer can make, even the optimal number of lectures a student can attend (which is almost certainly not all of them). However,

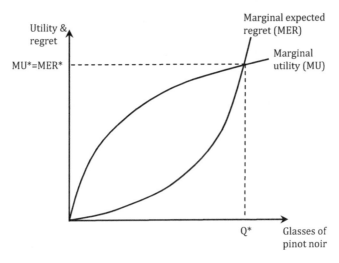

Figure 2.1 Marginal analysis and optimization

it represented the first step in the removal of psychology from economic analysis. Concern with the actual decision-making processes, psychological drivers and behaviours of us as individual players within the economy were, on the whole, quickly replaced with a single assumption: that we act *as if* optimizing our utility (or profit in the case of producers and return in the case of investors).

Marshall, however, was actually concerned with the drivers of our behaviour. He was particularly interested in how producers and consumers learn and its effects. He also examined the problem of managerial succession, hypothesizing that a business would eventually reach its maximum size because successors to the entrepreneur were bound to lose interest in it. Marshall's successors were sadly less concerned with such observations.

The marginal revolution, which was further entrenched in the works of subsequent economists – such as the work of Hicks and Allen on consumption (see Chapter 1) – firmly established Ricardo's rationalist approach as the accepted methodology for economists. Instead of studying the actual, real world, economists from this point on developed models of an artificial world in which everyone was assumed to behave as if they were optimizers. The key assumption governing economics since this time – rarely made explicit or spoken about – is that through understanding their artificial world, economists would learn valuable insights about the real world.

The emergence of "the master" (Skidelsky 2009)

If ever there was a case of the right thinker being in the right place at the right time, it was John Maynard Keynes (1883–1946). Born into an affluent and academically successful family in Cambridge – his father, John Neville Keynes had been one of Marshall's earliest students and rose to a professorship at Cambridge – John Maynard was encouraged to develop his intellect and curiosity from an early age. At the age of four and a half, he was already grappling with the meaning of interest: a concept that most children three times his age struggle with today. Keynes was educated at Eton College and then at the University of Cambridge, before living an adult life of exceptional variety, at one point or another working as a civil servant, a Cambridge professor, an advisor to the prime minister and a foreign envoy to the United States with the task of securing financial aid for the UK after the Second World War. Keynes also found time to pursue his aesthetic interests, establishing a theatre in Cambridge and acting as chairman of a governmental arts committee.

With the Wall Street Crash in October 1929, the developed world sunk into the Great Depression. The mainstream economic belief at the time – the "Treasury View" – was that economies would correct themselves. The argument was effectively that the increasing numbers of unemployed workers would start to offer themselves to employers for lower wages, which would depress businesses' costs of production, incentivizing entrepreneurs to expand their productions and to hire more workers, ultimately returning the economy to its natural state. The solution to the depression in the UK, then, was obvious: all that was needed was for the unemployed to accept lower wages. Simple. However, as Keynes repeatedly travelled between Cambridge and London he simply did not see any evidence of this happening. Wages were falling, but the queues at soup kitchens and the levels of everyday deprivation felt by ordinary people were increasing rather than contracting.

In 1936, Keynes published his most famous and influential work, *The General Theory of Employment, Interest and Money*. In this he argued there is no natural correction mechanism for an economy in recession. Far from being able to correct itself, an economy can easily become condemned to a perpetually depressed state. According to Keynes, at least a part of the reasoning for this lies in the psychology of everyone involved in an economy.

Business owners and entrepreneurs, for instance, do not make their production decisions according to the cold, logical analysis of data. They are instead driven by what Keynes called "animal spirits": by the internal urges we all have to act at times, even when the evidence does not support it. In the midst of a recession, wage rates may be falling as the unemployed compete with one another to secure jobs but this is unlikely to spur a businesswoman to expand her business if she is filled with pessimism when she considers the economy and thinks about its likely state one, two or three years ahead. She therefore chooses to take no action in the hope of just making it through. Without business expansion, no new jobs are created and the economy remains stuck in its depressed state. Business managers are likely to take advantage of the falling wage rates to cut the amounts they pay to their remaining workers, but with less take home pay, this simply means those fortunate enough to still be in work have to reduce their expenditures, which leads to further drops in the demand for the output of producers, levels of production and employment. The economy may not simply become stuck in a state of high unemployment; it may even slide further into depression.

Keynes's *General Theory* revolutionized economic thinking, being hailed as the handbook for a new era of government intervention, which lasted until the 1970s. It was also a step forward in bringing psychology back to the fore of economic theory. For Keynes, psychological factors and gut feelings were of central importance to the functioning of an economy. As such, and contrary to the aims of Adam Smith, economics cannot be approached in the same way as physics: economics "deals with motives, expectations, psychological uncertainties ... It is as though the fall of the apple to the ground depended on the apple's motives on whether it is worthwhile falling to the ground, and whether the ground wanted the apple to fall, and on mistaken calculations on the part of the apple as to how far it was from the centre of the earth" (J. M. Keynes in Johnson & Moggridge 1987: 297–300). He also considered the simplifying procedures we use when in situations in which we simply do not know how to respond, such as our inclination to copy others and to naively accept and extrapolate data from the past.

Keynes's notion of animal spirits was developed more fully in the separate works of George Katona and G. L. S. Shackle: the latter explicitly so (Earl 2017). Through his surveys of consumer confidence at the University of Michigan, Katona showed consumption demand depends on the willingness of us as consumers to spend money in addition to our ability to do so, which was already accepted. He also showed how cycles of boom and bust in an economy could be driven by shifts in our consumer confidence before any shifts in the confidence of producers. Shackle, on the other hand, was more concerned with the ways entrepreneurs make decisions. He proposed we use our imaginations to assess the possible outcomes of a decision because we do not have knowledge of the true probabilities. In his later work, Shackle went on to present a model of decision-making very similar to that of prospect theory (see Chapters 3 and 4), with us focusing on gains and losses relative to predetermined reference points and employing utility functions resembling that in Figure 3.1. In his model, though, we only focus on the most salient gain and the most salient loss of each option, ignoring all other possible outcomes as a way of simplifying the decision-making process (Shackle 1949).

Developments in the 1950s

During the 1950s further challenges were made to the assumptions on which economics had become based. The most significant of these was that of Herbert Simon (1916–2001). Born in Minnesota and graduating with undergraduate and doctoral degrees from the University of Chicago, Simon held roles as an academic economist, psychologist, computer scientist and philosopher at the University of Chicago, the Illinois Institute of Technology and the Carnegie Institute of Technology in Pittsburgh (Carnegie Mellon University since its merger with the Mellon Institute of Industrial Research in 1967).

The focus of much of Simon's work was how we as individuals, and business organizations, actually make decisions. Perhaps the most important of his contributions came whilst he was at Carnegie, working in collaboration with a number of other notable economists – including John Muth, Charles Holt and Franco Modigliani – on a project looking at business decision-making. If one ever wants an example of how different conclusions can be drawn from the same set of information, this project is it. Muth's work on the project led him to assert that we do not just act as if we are optimizing, we actually do so with the same degree of accuracy and speed as economic analysts, econometricians and policy-makers. As a consequence, the notion of *rational expectations* was introduced to the discipline. In the starkest of contrasts, Simon's involvement in the project led him to propose that we are characterised by *bounded rationality* (see Chapter 4). Far from acting as if we optimize, we content ourselves with *satisficing*, with making decisions that are *good enough*, because we simply do not possess the cognitive ability to make optimal decisions. Simon also asserted we employ *heuristics* – simplifying rules of thumb – to help us as we make our decisions: an important precursor to the works that were to follow.

An argument can be made for Simon being the most badly treated economist in the history of the subject.[6] That two such incompatible views arose in the same department at the same time created a level of tension there that eventually led Simon to relocate to the department of psychology (Sent 1997). And more widely, far from welcoming the theory of bounded rationality as it had welcomed that of rational expectations, the economics profession as a whole has at various times and in various guises sought to sideline Simon's work. Despite being recognised with the 1978 Nobel Prize in economics, Simon lamented, "my economist friends have long since given up on me, consigning me to psychology or some other distant wasteland" (Simon 1991: 385). And this sidelining appears to be continuing, with both Simon and his work on bounded rationality often being consigned to the footnotes in the burgeoning literature on behavioural economics, if they are included at all. The famous *New York Times* article announcing the arrival of the discipline by Louis Uchitelle, for example, failed to refer to either Simon or his work (Uchitelle 2001).

Simon's work was further developed in the 1960s, particularly in application to decision-making within businesses. Richard Cyert and James March, also at the Carnegie Institute of Technology, examined the simple decision rules used by managers and Harvey Leibenstein introduced the notion of *x-inefficiency*. This latter theory is based on the simple observation that businesses are collections of individuals. Rather than seeking to maximize the efficiency and profit level of their business, workers actually seek to maximize their own welfare, balancing the reward that arises from increasing their effort with the criticism it induces from fellow workers concerned about being shown-up. The less-than-maximum effort that results creates a level of inefficiency in a business: x-inefficiency.

At the same time, Vernon Smith – along with a number of others – was pioneering the use of laboratory experiments in economics (Library of Economics and Liberty 2008). Most economists up until this time had maintained the view that conducting experiments was simply not an appropriate, or rigorous, methodology for their discipline. Smith led the challenge to this, initially using small-scale experiments as a teaching tool within his lectures at Purdue University – which eventually led to his ground-breaking publication of 1962, showing that a free market can indeed converge to an equilibrium outcome – but then expanding his research programme to investigate settings such as the outcomes of different auction types and the ways people actually solve the free-riding problem in public goods games (see Chapter 6). Holding professorship positions at a number of American universities throughout his career, Smith is largely responsible for the establishment of experimental economics as a distinct field and for many of the findings within this book, which are derived from the experimental methods he pioneered: for which he shared the 2002 Nobel Prize in economics.

Finally, computational limitations were also integrated into the models of mainstream economics in the form of additional, cognitive constraints to optimization during this period. A literature concerned with optimal decision rules began to expand and mainstream economists were able to push psychological concerns to one side again. This also represented the point at which the literature on bounded rationality diverged from that on behavioural economics: the former being concerned with analysing our cognitive limitations as constraints in models of optimization and the latter being concerned with understanding our actual decision-making processes (Earl 2017).

Modern behavioural economics

In the 1970s, Daniel Kahneman and Amos Tversky expanded decision-making experiments into a range of real life scenarios that had not been examined before. With findings pertaining to anchoring, framing and the effects of defaults and decoys (see Chapter 6), the difference between actual behaviour and that predicted by the models of mainstream economics became evermore significant. The need for economics and psychology to be brought back together became increasingly clear and the modern discipline of behavioural economics was born. In the 1980s, the Russell Sage Foundation sponsored a behavioural economics round table, attended by many of those whose work is examined in this book: Richard Thaler, Colin Camerer, Matthew Rabin, David Laibson, Sendhil Mullainathan and George Loewenstein (in addition to Kahneman and Tversky).

However, although the Kahneman and Tversky view has become the dominant school of behavioural economics, it is certainly not the only one. Kahneman and Tversky have asserted that the decision-making heuristics we employ result in us being biased and making errors of judgement. Gerd Gigerenzer – a German psychologist at the Max Planck Institute for Human Development in Berlin – and his colleagues make a contradictory assertion: our decision-making heuristics actually make us smart, enabling us to make superior choices.

SUMMARY

- To the founders of modern economics, such as Adam Smith and Thomas Malthus, the study of economics was indistinguishable from that of psychology.
- The pursuit of scientific rigour led to the marginal revolution at the beginning of the twentieth century, which established optimization at the heart of economic analysis. Psychological concerns were pushed to one side.
- The contributions of John Maynard Keynes served to highlight for a time the importance of psychology for understanding our behaviour, which were developed by George Katona and G. L. S. Shackle.
- In the 1950s and 1960s, a number of economic thinkers – such as Herbert Simon, Richard Cyert, James March and Harvey Leibenstein – challenged the mainstream assumptions about our decision-making, particularly that within businesses.
- Starting in the 1950s, Vernon Smith was a key pioneer of the use of experiments in economics, opening the door to modern behavioural economics.
- Modern behavioural economics emerged in the 1980s, emphasizing the biases and errors view of Kahneman and Tversky.

Notes

1. The importance of Daniel Kahneman and Amos Tversky in the field cannot be overstated. Tversky would almost certainly have been co-recipient of the Nobel Prize in economics in 2002, but had sadly passed away in 1996.

2. Although only these three have been explicitly awarded for works relating to behavioural economics, there are claims that those awarded to George Akerlof and Joseph Stiglitz in 2001 can also be claimed by the field: see Frantz (2004).

3. For a thorough discussion of Adam Smith's life and works, and of those of many of the other economic thinkers in this chapter, see Heilbroner (2000).

4. The Physiocrats viewed human society as a natural web of life, with its members engaging in a determined set of interactions that ultimately balanced the system. Their *tableau économique* was essentially the precursor to the circular flow of income taught in the first lesson of any introductory economics course.

5. Alfred Marshall, having been "Second Wrangler" (scoring the second highest First in the Cambridge mathematics tripos) rose to the position of Professor of Political Economy at the University of Cambridge. The economics library at Cambridge is still named in his honour. As a result of the university's strict rules about celibacy, Marshall had to leave when he married his student and co-author Mary Paley in 1877. He became the first Principal at University College, Bristol (which later became the University of Bristol).

6. The other leading contender for this unwanted accolade is Lorie Tarshis: see Harcourt (1995).

3

Preferences

One of the aspects of our behaviour that we now understand considerably more because of behavioural economics is that of our *preferences*: the values we assign to the various options available to us when making decisions. The view of preferences traditionally adopted by mainstream economists is that they are *complete, stable, reflexive, transitive* and *immune from changes in ownership* (see Chapter 1), but there now exists a plethora of behavioural findings demonstrating they are not in fact like this.

These findings are the focus of this chapter. Our preferences when faced with immediate choices – which may or may not be certain – are examined first, leaving our preferences when faced with choices across time to later in the chapter. The focus throughout is on the decisions we make that are not affected by, nor affect, the decisions of others: the focus is on our individual rather than strategic behaviour (see Chapter 5 for an examination of the latter).

Loss aversion

Jimmy Connors, the former world number one tennis player with eight major championship titles to his name, remarked that he hates to lose more than he likes to win. Such a sentiment is perhaps unsurprising from such a competitive individual, but behavioural economists have in fact shown it to be common to us all: a sentiment known as *loss aversion*.

The traditional assumption that our preferences are reflexive (see Chapter 1) implies the utility we gain from an item is exactly the same as the utility we lose from having the very same item taken away from us. Work on *prospect theory* (see Chapter 4), however, reveals this is not the case and that our preferences can in fact be represented by utility functions such as that in Figure 3.1. Gaining an item – a first glass of wine in this case – brings us a certain amount of utility, in this case an amount of satisfaction equivalent to £5. Gaining a second brings us additional utility, but less than the first because of *diminishing marginal utility* (see Chapter 2): £2 in this case. Having a first glass of wine taken away from us, however, reduces our utility by more than we benefitted from gaining a first glass – by £6, for example – and losing a second glass reduces our utility by more than gaining a second glass increased it, in this case by £2.50. As Kahneman and Tversky explain, "A salient characteristic of attitudes to changes in welfare is that losses loom larger than gains. The aggravation that one experiences in losing a sum of money appears to be greater than the pleasure associated with gaining the same amount" (Kahneman & Tversky 1979: 279). This is loss aversion.

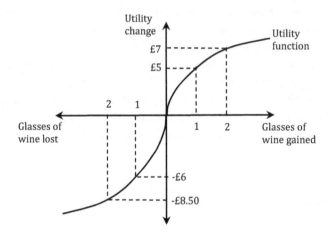

Figure 3.1 Loss aversion

That our utility functions are sigmoid shaped, as in Figure 3.1, leads to a couple of lessons about how we should deliver news. Looking at the diagram, two separate pieces of bad news are felt by the receiver as a total loss of £12, whereas one double piece of bad news is felt as a total loss of only £8.50. With bad news, it is better to deliver it all in one go rather than to spread it out. Conversely, two separate pieces of good news are felt as a total gain of £10, whereas a double piece of good news is felt as a total gain of £7. With good news, it is better to deliver it a bit at a time. This logic underlies the reason for sellers of "big ticket items", such as cars, giving small cash rebates to their customers. An individual who has just purchased a new hatchback for £21,000 and then receives £500 back from the dealership as a "gift" feels a higher overall welfare than an identical individual who has just purchased the same vehicle for £20,500. The utility effect of the £500 cost reduction is marginal when the total cost is initially £21,000, whereas the utility effect of a £500 gift is considerable when no gift is expected.

The endowment effect

That our utility functions resemble that in Figure 3.1 also leads to our behaviour being characterized by the *endowment effect* (Thaler 1980). Perhaps the most well known demonstration of this is the laboratory "mug experiment" (Kahneman *et al.* 1990). Undergraduate students sitting on alternating seats in classes at Cornell and Simon Fraser Universities were given university-branded coffee mugs, which they were invited to sell to their peers in the class in a variety of experimental rounds. The students were instructed to record the prices at which they would either be willing to sell a mug or to buy one, being aware that any of the mutually acceptable trades could be enforced and they would have to actually transfer their mugs for money. The median recorded selling price of mugs was more than twice the median recorded buying price. This has become an established result: we tend to value an item twice as much if we believe it belongs to us than if we do not believe it to be ours.

This study has since been taken into the real world (Ariely 2012). Half of the 76 participants in the experiment – 30 of whom were car sales people and 46 estate agents – were given mugs before being asked for what price they would each be willing to sell them. The remaining half of the participants were each asked what amount they would be willing to spend to buy a mug. The reported price of the former was found to be approximately three times that of the latter.

In contradiction to the standard view of preferences outlined in Chapter 1, our preferences are determined by our sense of ownership. Altering the ownership of an item causes our preferences, and so our behaviour, to change.

The status quo bias

Loss aversion also causes our behaviour to be characterized by *status quo bias*, which refers to our tendency to be reluctant to move away from the situation in which we find ourselves. This is because the potential losses from such a move appear to us much greater than the potential gains (Samuelson & Zeckhauser 1988). The initial work on this involved MBA and undergraduate students at Boston and Harvard Universities responding to hypothetical scenarios in which they had to identify which of a range of investments they would make. From a range of experimental settings, investments became substantially more popular when they were identified as the status quo option. And the strength of this effect increased when the number of available options from which the students had to choose was expanded. The excessive choice effect magnifies our status quo bias (see Chapter 1).

Subsequent field experiments have served to confirm this behavioural bias. In one survey, for example, Californian electricity consumers were divided into two groups: the service reliability, but also the cost, for those in one group being much greater than for those in the other (Hartman *et al.* 1991). When asked to state their preferences about reliability-charge combinations, 60 per cent of respondents in each group expressed a preference to remain with their current providers and only 6 per cent in each expressed a desire to switch to the reliability-charge combination provided to the other group (see also Kahneman *et al.* 1991).

The existence of the effect has also been established, perhaps more starkly, in situations involving very real, physical pain and anxiety. Building on psychological studies that show individuals prefer to shorten the waiting time before they experience an electric shock, one study tested whether or not subjects in a situation such as this are susceptible to this bias (Suri *et al.* 2013). 41 student participants were told they were each going to experience an electric shock, calibrated to the highest intensity they could each bear, at an unspecified point during each of 14 experimental trials. They were then divided into two groups. Those in one group were able to reduce the time they had to wait for their shocks by ten seconds simply by pressing a button. Those in the other had to make a choice between two buttons, one of which would reduce the waiting time by ten seconds whilst the other would leave the waiting time to be randomly chosen. Those in the latter group, in which there was no established status quo option as they had to press a button, chose to shorten their wait 75 per cent of the time. Their counterparts in the former group, in which the randomly chosen wait time was established as the status quo, chose to do so only 41 per cent of the time. In a second experiment, the process was repeated with 40 students, but with the choice being whether or not to reduce the probability of receiving an electric shock at all by 90 per cent. On this occasion, those in the group in which no status quo was established chose to reduce the probability of receiving shocks 85 per cent of the time, whereas those in the group in which there was a status quo option chose to do so only 52 per cent of the time. In both scenarios, particularly the latter, participants chose to retain a status quo option even when it was unambiguously less attractive than the available alternative. This perhaps explains the rates of medical non-compliance – of citizens failing to follow specific medical advice – which in developed countries are as high as 50 per cent and in the United States are responsible for 10 per cent of hospital admissions.

As a direct consequence of our, often exaggerated, fear of loss and our preference for inaction over action (known as *omission predisposition*), we have a tendency to choose not to change the situation in which we find ourselves even when the alternative is demonstrably better, even less physically painful. How often do we choose, perhaps subconsciously, not to change our mobile phone, insurance or banking provider even though we know there is a superior alternative available?

The reflection effect

A third effect on our behaviour of loss aversion is the *reflection effect*. When we find ourselves in a situation in which we are gaining something and so are in the top right-hand quadrant of Figure 3.1 – meaning we are in the *domain of gain* – we are reluctant to take a risk regarding the number of items we gain. This is because the amount our utility increase rises from gaining an additional glass of wine, in this case, is less than the amount our utility increase falls from losing a glass. However, when we find ourselves in a situation in which we are losing something and so are in the bottom left-hand quadrant – and so are in the *domain of loss* – taking such a risk is appealing because the reduction in our utility loss from having one less glass taken away from us is greater than the increase in our utility loss from having an additional glass taken away. We are *risk averse* in the domain of gain but *risk seeking* in the domain of loss. This is the reflection effect.

This effect has been observed in the investment choices of American chartered financial analysts (Olsen 1997), which essentially replicates the "Asian disease problem" (see Chapter 6). A group of analysts were asked to choose between the two investment options in each of the two settings shown in Table 3.1, both of which relate to a client who has previously made a $60,000 investment. Not much inspection is required to identify that the two sets of options are identical, just with those in the first setting being phrased (or *framed*: see Chapter 6) in terms of gain and those in the second being phrased in terms of loss. Being the same, the standard economic view asserts that those who select option 1.1 will also select option 2.1, whilst those who select option 1.2 will also select option 2.2. In the study, however, 65 per cent of respondents chose option 1.1 and 35 per cent chose option 1.2, but then 32 per cent chose option 2.1 and 68 per cent option 2.2. Not only does this demonstrate the reflection effect, it also demonstrates *preference reversal*: the effect that we change our choice despite the options not actually being altered in any meaningful way, violating the mainstream assumptions that our preferences are reflexive and stable.

The reflection effect has more recently been observed in the wake of the January 2011 floods in Brisbane, Australia. 220 residential homeowners in

Table 3.1 Investment options and the reflection effect

Setting One	
	Outcome
Option 1.1	$20,000 of the client's investment will be saved
Option 1.2	A one-third probability that $60,000 of the client's investment will be saved and a two-third probability that $0 of the client's investment will be saved
Setting Two	
	Outcome
Option 2.1	$40,000 of the client's investment will be lost
Option 2.2	A one-third probability that $0 of the client's investment will be lost and a two-third probability that $60,000 of the client's investment will be lost

the affected area were surveyed about the impact of the flooding and their opinions about the response of the authorities. As a reward for completing the questionnaire, the respondents were able to choose between a $10 cash payment on the one hand and a lottery scratch card with a face value of $10 and a potential prize of $500,000 on the other. Fifty per cent of respondents owning homes 0.75 metres above the peak level of the flood – and so had been unaffected – chose the scratch card compared to 75 per cent of those owning homes 0.75 metres below the peak level of the flood – and so had been affected. Those experiencing loss were 50 per cent more willing to accept risk (Page *et al.* 2014).

That our behaviour is dependent on the perceived gain and loss domains in which we find ourselves has important implications. It has been suggested, for example, that the reflection effect explains why medical patients tend to choose increasingly risky treatments as their conditions decline (Raisel *et al.* 2005). This has stark implications for how medical practitioners should provide information to patients: they possess the power to determine a patient's feeling of gain or loss and so can inadvertently manipulate his or her choice of treatment.

Ambiguity aversion and seeking

QUESTION: *Two urns each contain ten balls. In the first urn there are five red balls and five black balls. In the second, the proportions of the two colours are unknown. You are faced with the four possible payments shown in Table 3.2, each contingent on the lottery you choose and the colour of the ball you draw. Rank the four lotteries according to your order of preference.*

Table 3.2 The two-colour Ellsberg paradox

	Urn with 50/50 proportions		Urn with unknown proportions	
	Red is drawn	Black is drawn	Red is drawn	Black is drawn
Lottery 1	£10	£0		
Lottery 2			£10	£0
Lottery 3	£0	£10		
Lottery 4			£0	£10

This problem is known as the two-colour Ellsberg paradox (Ellsberg 1961). It is a paradox because we tend to have no preference between lotteries 1 and 3, or between lotteries 2 and 4, but to prefer both lotteries 1 and 3 to both lotteries 2 and 4. This is irrational because the expected payment from each of the two urns is exactly the same: across the two lotteries in each case £10 will be paid whichever colour is drawn.

That we inherently dislike the urn with unknown proportions has become known as *ambiguity aversion*. Ambiguity refers to settings in which the probabilities of the possible outcomes are not known for sure, which is different to risk, which refers to settings in which the precise outcome is unknown but the probabilities of the possibilities are known with certainty. Such ambiguity can arise because of either missing or conflicting information (see Trautmann & van de Kuilen 2015).

This experiment, and the slightly more sophisticated three-urn variation, has repeatedly shown us – whether students or non-students, from Western countries or not, and adults or children – to be ambiguity averse. However, this result appears to be dependent on whether the lotteries involve gains or losses and whether the outcomes have a high or low likelihood. In certain settings we actually prefer ambiguity: behaviour known as *ambiguity seeking*. The fourfold pattern shown in Table 3.3 appears to describe our behaviour when we find ourselves in ambiguous situations.

Table 3.3 Situations of ambiguity aversion and ambiguity seeking

	Gains	Losses
High likelihood outcome	Ambiguity aversion	Ambiguity seeking
Low likelihood outcome	Ambiguity seeking	Ambiguity aversion

Such behaviour has also been confirmed in real-life settings. In the initial phase of a marketing-related study, for example, the quality levels of a range of brands were established as being ambiguous to different degrees. Consumers were then tested for the strengths of their ambiguity aversion before being asked to choose amongst the different brands. The study found, perhaps unsurprisingly albeit reassuringly, that the more ambiguity-averse consumers tended to prefer the low ambiguity brands (Muthukrishnan *et al.* 2009). The importance of ambiguity aversion has also been demonstrated in a number of development settings. Farmers in both Peru and Laos who avoided ambiguity in an experimental task, for example, were shown to be less likely to adopt new crop varieties (see Engle-Warnick *et al.* 2007; Ross *et al.* 2012). Ambiguity aversion can actually lead to poverty in such settings because it causes people to refuse possibly profitable economic opportunities (Cardenas & Carpenter 2013).

The discounted utility model

Would you prefer to receive a gift of £100 today or in exactly a year from now? The standard view in economics about how we make decisions across time such as this – decisions about actions we are to take today, tomorrow or at any time in the future (also known as *intertemporal decision-making*) – is that of the *discounted utility model*. Proposed in 1937, this model suggests we prefer to receive a gift today: that future values appear smaller to us (Samuelson 1937). A £100 in a year from now is worth less to us than £100 today. This model has been typically implemented in the form of exponential discounting, which assumes we employ a discount rate to reduce the value of options in the future that is both constant throughout time – meaning we reduce the value of an option by a fixed percentage each period – and for all different types of choice.

The analytical power of this model has been proven repeatedly in the 80 years since its conception, being undeniably simple and employable in the analysis of a range of different settings. However, since the early 1980s its descriptive power – its realism – has been challenged by an ever-expanding body of empirical evidence, which has led to a number of alternative descriptions of our intertemporal preferences (see Frederick *et al.* 2002).

Hyperbolic discounting

QUESTION 1: *What value gift would you require in one month from now, in a year from now and in ten years from now, in order for you to be indifferent between each of those gifts and a gift of £15 today?*

QUESTION 2: *Would you prefer to receive £100 today or £110 tomorrow? What about the choice between £100 in 30 days from now and £110 in 31 days from now?*

The first, and most documented, violation of the discounted utility model is that our real-life behaviour reveals we employ discount rates that decline over time. When respondents are asked to answer Question 1 above, their median responses tend to be around £20, £50 and £100. This implies an average annual discount rate of 345 per cent over a single month, 120 per cent over a year and 19 per cent over ten years: a declining discount rate (Thaler 1981). Experiments using Question 2 demonstrate we tend to choose £110 in 31 days rather than £100 in 30 days; but we tend to choose £100 today over £110 tomorrow. A sequence of similar questions were asked of 14 Harvard University summer school students, with a mean age of 18.2 years. All 14 students consistently reversed their preferences, from the smaller, less delayed reward to the larger, greater delayed reward as the time between the present day and the pair of options increased. The amounts can be the same in different cases, as can the length of the delays between options, but we reveal different preferences depending on the timing of the option pairs. We become less and less impatient the farther into the future the options lie, which violates the standard assumption of our preferences being stable (Kirby & Herrnstein 1995).

That we employ a declining discount rate is included in the alternative model of our intertemporal behaviour known as *hyperbolic* discounting. This has been used effectively to explain a number of cases of our seemingly irrational behaviour. That many of us frequently engage in credit card borrowing at high rates of interest suggests we employ double-digit discount rates when considering the future repayments we will have to make. That we accumulate relatively large amounts of wealth at low interest rates for retirement – by investing in property, for example – implies we employ single-digit discount rates for the future financial rewards these investments will bring (Laibson *et al.* 2003). The times we have committed ourselves to gym memberships and diet regimes in order to attain future health benefits suggest we only marginally discount these future benefits. But our apparent inability to resist the unhealthy meal that same evening suggests we discount the future health rewards greatly in comparison to the immediate gratification the meal will bring. Our behaviour is unstable across time.

Alternative models of intertemporal decision-making

Hyperbolic-discounting models are not the only explanations that have been put forward to explain our time-inconsistent behaviour, although they are the most prominent. At least two competing models have also been advocated. The first is an application of the procedural approach associated with both prospect theory and mental accounting (see Chapter 4). This postulates that we go through a three-stage simplifying procedure when making choices between options at different moments in time (Rubinstein 2003). When answering the questions about receiving either £100 today or £110 tomorrow and £100 in 30 days from now or £110 in 31 days from now, we:

1. Look for *dominance* between the two options. If in each case the reward involving a shorter wait time is greater than that involving the greater wait, the decision is straightforward: the first option would be preferred on both counts to the second.
2. Look for *similarities* between the two rewards and between the two wait times. If we consider the two rewards in a given setting to be the same, we simply make the decision based on our preference regarding the wait times: we choose the option with the shortest wait. And vice versa in situations in which we consider the two wait times to be the same.
3. Make the decision based on a different criterion if neither of the first two steps has been decisive.

The apparent inconsistency in our decisions when faced with these two problems, then, is easily explained by such a procedural approach: it is likely that we consider a 30-day wait to be essentially the same as the 31-day wait, and so we naturally choose to wait the additional day for the higher reward. The second type of model used to explain our behaviour in such situations is based on the idea that we are composed of two selves. One of our selves is a long-sighted "planner" whilst the other is a myopic "doer". Our behaviour is simply determined by the interaction of, and competition between, these two selves (see, for example, Thaler & Shefrin 1981, and Fudenberg & Levine 2006). Although such procedural and two-self models have not been as popular amongst economists as those of hyperbolic discounting, they are favoured by psychologists who see in them much greater psychological worth.

SUMMARY

- We feel the negative effects of a loss much more acutely than the positive effects of a gain of equal magnitude: we are *loss averse*.
- We tend to assign a greater value to an item if we believe it is ours than if we do not possess it: the ownership of an item affects its value. This is known as the *endowment effect*.
- We tend to be reluctant to move away from the situation in which we find ourselves because the potential loss from doing so often looms larger than the associated potential gain: we are characterised by *status quo bias*.
- We tend to be risk seeking when we perceive ourselves to be in a situation of loss and to be risk averse when we perceive ourselves to be in a situation of gain: this is the *reflection effect*.
- We discount the value of outcomes in the future using a discount rate that declines over time: this is known as *hyperbolic discounting*.

4

Processes

Popular books on behavioural economics, many of which enliven a growing proportion of the economics shelf space in any good bookshop, tend to focus on the findings about our preferences explored in the previous chapter. However, behavioural economics is much broader than just this: it is also concerned with uncovering the actual processes we execute when making our decisions. This work does not contradict that of mainstream economists, who have largely been unconcerned with the *means* by which we make decisions, being solely concerned with the *ends* and their effects. In this sense, behavioural economics is a welcome extension of the economics discipline: welcome because an understanding of the processes involved in our decision-making is essential if the decisions we make across the differing settings in which we find ourselves are to be in any way predictable. The ends cannot be understood in isolation from the means.

Bounded rationality and satisficing

Since the beginning of the twentieth century, mainstream economists have at least implicitly assumed that we make our decisions optimally (see Chapters 1 and 2). The polymath psychologist, computer scientist and Noble Prize winning economist Herbert Simon saw things very differently, arguably being the first to focus on the actual procedures involved in our decision-making. He suggested we are characterized by *bounded rationality*: that in all but the very basic and most straightforward of settings we are simply unable to make optimal decisions.

Consider the relatively unimpressive decision involved in purchasing a bottle of whisky as a gift, for example. Depending on our budget and the degree of refinement of the recipient's taste, we can with relative ease narrow down our choice to that between single malts or between blends; but then we have to consider the desired intensities of peat and smoke that can be tasted, the age of the spirit, whether we opt for normal or cask strength, the prestige of the distillery, the appearance of the bottle and the price. To make this decision optimally requires us to look at every bottle available to us – which could be in a whole array of different shops in our local town as well as on an increasing number of websites online – comparing them all according to each of these characteristics. A seemingly unimpressive decision on the surface, but one that actually requires an amount of cognitive processing that can only be deemed heroic. Witnessing business decisions of much greater consequence than this first hand, Simon observed we are subject to two unyielding forces. On the one hand, even relatively straightforward decisions such as this are characterized by high levels of complexity, usually involving multitudes of relevant pieces of information that need to be carefully considered if the optimal choice is to be identified. And on the other, our cognitive capacities to process such information are physiologically limited. Simon likened these forces to two blades of a pair of scissors, which together make it almost impossible for us to make decisions in the optimal manner traditionally assumed by economists. These are the blades of bounded rationality.

Instead of striving for optimal decisions, then, Simon suggested we content ourselves with *satisficing*: with making decisions that are just good enough. Rather than examining every available bottle of whisky before making our choice, we reach for our wallets as soon as we find one that meets our, often subconscious, predetermined criteria. We then dive into the closest pub or coffee shop for a well earned drink, being unconcerned about our suspicion that there is a superior bottle of whisky on sale in one of the shops farther down the street. More formally, we possess *aspiration levels* – minimum conditions that need to be met for us to be satisfied – regarding each element of the decision at hand and we engage in a search process until we find a choice that satisfies each of those aspirations.

Consider again the decision examined in Figure 1.2, in which we have to make a choice about the combination of two goods to buy (also represented in Figure 4.1). The analysis within mainstream economics assumes we act as if we look at each and every possible option and then choose the one lying on the highest indifference curve we can afford (option X in Figure 4.1). Instead of making the decision as if like this, Simon suggested we actually

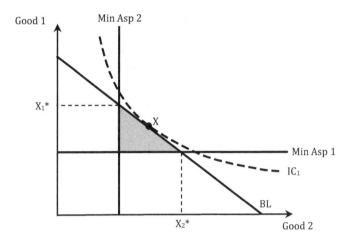

Figure 4.1 Satisficing

approach it with an existing idea of the minimum amounts of the goods with which we would be satisfied: "Min Asp 1" and "Min Asp 2", respectively. Our decision-making is then the infinitely simpler procedure of searching through the available options until we find one that both satisfies these two criteria and is affordable: any option lying within the shaded triangle in the diagram.

That we are characterized by bounded rationality is the first half of the explanation for much of our consumption behaviour that seems irrational from the view of mainstream economics. It is well documented, for instance, that we exhibit ranges of price insensitivity when making our daily purchases. The price of everyday goods can change quite significantly and yet we simply accept the resulting reduction in value for money because the deal remains good enough. It is also well documented that we are reluctant to switch utility providers even though by not doing so we are usually hit by substantial increases in the tariffs we pay: again partly because the new terms "will do".

Prospect theory

Prospect theory – more formally *cumulative prospect theory*: an updated version of the original model – is by far the most influential behavioural model of our decision-making, focusing on our decisions between prospects, or bundles of probabilistic outcomes. For example, the choice between one option that results in £150 with 50 per cent probability and £0 with 50 per cent probability, and another option that results in £110 with 45 per cent probability and £50 with 55 per cent probability, is a choice between two prospects (Kahneman & Tversky 1979; Tversky & Kahneman 1992). Prospect theory makes three major contributions:

1. We make decisions by evaluating the available options relative to pre-determined *reference points* rather than by evaluating them according to their absolute values.
2. We employ a whole range of *heuristics*, or rules of thumb, to make the decision-making process simpler.
3. We are affected by the losses we incur very differently to the way we are affected by the gains we make, even if they are of equal absolute magnitudes: we exhibit *loss aversion* (see Chapter 3).

Prospect theory conceives of our decision-making as consisting of two distinct stages: an *editing* phase and an *evaluation* phase. Building on the notion of bounded rationality, according to this theory we first subconsciously edit each of the available options, making them easier for us to understand and evaluate. There are six steps to this, shown in Figure 4.2. To illustrate these steps, consider the situation in which you have previously paid £1 to enter a prize draw and your number has been pulled from the hat. For your prize, you are able to choose one of the following two lottery tickets. Which would you choose?

TICKET 1: A 61 per cent chance of winning a bottle of champagne sold in the shop for £49.99, a 38 per cent chance of winning £101 cash, and a 1 per cent chance of winning a £250 shopping voucher for each of the next ten months.

TICKET 2: A 50 per cent chance of winning a box of chocolates sold in the shop for £19.99, a 19 per cent chance of winning a wine selection sold in the shop for £318.99; and a 31 per cent chance of winning a cake sold in the shop for £19.99.

Step 1: coding. Rather than taking the outcomes of the available options at face value and in absolute terms, we tend to denominate them as gains or

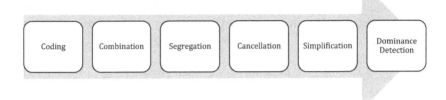

Figure 4.2 The steps of prospect theory

losses relative to predetermined reference points. Consider the bottle of champagne that could be won with Ticket 1, for example. If we had to purchase this for ourselves, we may actually be willing to pay at most £35 for it, but we assign it a value of £49.99 because we have been told this is its current price in the shop. Instead of viewing it in terms of its absolute worth to us, we view it as a gain of £49.99.

Step 2: combination. As the first step in making these options easier to understand, we combine prospects with identical outcomes. As such, we actually view Ticket 2 as offering us the possibilities of winning something worth £19.99 with 81 per cent probability and winning something worth £318.99 with 19 per cent probability.

Step 3: segregation. We identify and disregard outcomes that are certain. With Ticket 1, for example, we are guaranteed to win £49.99 and so we view this choice as one that simply gives us a 38 per cent chance of winning an additional £51.01 and a 1 per cent chance of winning an additional £2,450.01. With Ticket 2, on the other hand, we are guaranteed to win £19.99 and so this choice simply gives us a 19 per cent chance of winning an additional £299.

Step 4: simplification. This involves us making probabilities and outcomes more straightforward to comprehend by rounding them and assigning zero values to outcomes with very low probabilities. With Ticket 1, then, we have a 40 per cent chance of winning £50 in addition to the guaranteed £50, whereas with Ticket 2 we have a 20 per cent chance of winning £300 in addition to the guaranteed £20.

From these four steps of editing, Ticket 1 offers us an expected gain of £70. Ticket 2, on the other hand, offers an expected gain of £80. The latter is clearly to be preferred. When calculated mathematically, however, the expected return from Ticket 1 is actually £93.87 whilst that from Ticket 2 is £76.80. The editing process has reversed the preference ordering of the two options. Importantly, this is not only because the very low probability of winning £2,500 from Ticket 1 is disregarded: the value of Ticket 2 is also increased through the editing phase.

In addition to these four editing steps, there are also those of *cancellation* and *dominance detection*. Cancellation involves us disregarding identical components across the options. In the example here, both options have included the £1 cost of the prize draw coupon. As this is common to both possible outcomes, we simply ignore it as being irrelevant. Similarly, dominance detection entails us identifying common outcomes across the options and comparing them solely according to their probabilities. This does not play a role in this case.

Once we have edited the available prospects – and so have valued them according to the gains and losses they represent relative to our reference points – we then assign them utility values using Figure 3.1. It is at this point the second phase of the process kicks in, and we evaluate the prospects before making our choices. This final phase involves us replacing the actual probability that each prospect will occur with a decision weight, which we do because we find it difficult to interpret probabilities correctly. During this phase we tend to over-weigh any small probabilities compared to those with zero probability (called *subadditivity*) and to under-weigh high probabilities compared to those that are certain (called *subcertainty*). This means a 10 per cent increase in the probability of a prospect has a greater impact on our decision-making when it changes the probability from either 0 per cent to 10 per cent or from 90 per cent to 100 per cent than it does when it increases the probability from either 30 per cent to 40 per cent or 60 per cent to 70 per cent. And so this causes us to behave differently to the predictions in mainstream economics depending on whether prospects are highly likely to occur (which we view as being more risky than they actually are) or unlikely to occur (which we view as being less risky than they actually are) in addition to whether their outcomes are gains or losses (because of the nature of our utility function in Figure 3.1): as outlined in Table 4.1. This phase is not needed in our running example because once we have chosen a ticket it is certain we will receive it: the two prospects are each certain.

Table 4.1 Situations of risk aversion and risk seeking

		The nature of the outcomes	
		Gains	Losses
Probability	High but not certain	Risk aversion	Risk seeking
Size	Low but not impossible	Risk seeking	Risk aversion

Mental accounting

At some point in each of our lives – perhaps during our years as a student or as a low-paid employee – we have probably all experimented with managing our finances by setting out a number of tins, assigning each tin to a type of expenditure, and then dividing our money across the tins according to the amount we allocated to each expenditure type. These tins may have been actual, physical receptacles kept on our kitchen counter or on a shelf in our bedroom; but they may equally have been pages in a notebook or rows in a spreadsheet. Either way, the process involved us allocating the money we had available across the competing things for which it could be used. By subsequently refusing to spend more on a given type of expenditure than the amount we allocated to it, this process probably helped us to roughly make best use of our limited budgets and to discipline ourselves against the risk of spending too much on a luxury item and then running out of funds needed for food.

This is precisely the process involved in the mental accounting model of decision-making, for which there is a burgeoning amount of supporting evidence (Thaler 1985 & 1999). This model conceives of our financial decision-making as consisting of three distinct elements: *assignment, evaluation* and *choice bracketing*.

We first, often subconsciously, assign our funds to specific accounts for our different types of expenditure: for example, groceries, utilities, clothing, entertainment and eating out. We tend to make this a malleable procedure, deliberately establishing a miscellaneous account that can be used for small and routine expenses, such as the bar of chocolate we buy when filling our car with petrol (the latter probably coming from a specific account for fuel). Evidence suggests, however, the amounts we allocate to different accounts are not *fungible*, meaning they are not perfectly substitutable for one another. This can lead to seemingly irrational purchase choices. Evidence also suggests poorer individuals and households tend to set their accounts for shorter time periods.

We also assign different sources of income to different accounts, thereby earmarking them for different types of expenditure. We tend to distribute the additional income we receive from a pay rise across all our accounts, enabling us to spend more on groceries but also more on entertainment and dining. Upon receiving a lump-sum rebate from the taxman, however, it is much more likely that we will view this as a gift and so spend it all on a luxury item, separate from our usual accounting process.

When deliberating about a financial decision, we then evaluate the available options in the way proposed in prospect theory: as gains and losses relative to predetermined reference points rather than in absolute terms, to which we assign utility values corresponding to Figure 3.1. There is strong empirical support for the proposition that in evaluating options we do so to maximize our own utility, following the logic of delivering news in Chapter 3: we segregate gains, integrate losses, integrate small losses with larger gains, and segregate small gains from larger losses. This is called *hedonic editing*.

We also evaluate possible purchases according to two distinct types of utility. On the one hand there is *acquisition utility*, which is the amount we actually value an item above what we pay for it (also known as *consumer surplus*). On the other is *transaction utility*, which refers to the perceived value of the deal: the difference between what we expect to pay for an item and what we actually pay. Separating the overall utility from purchasing an item into these two components leads to an explanation for the products we buy on a whim and then never use (the waffle maker gathering dust on the kitchen worktop perhaps) and those that would enhance our lives but we never buy (possibly the fancy food processor). In the first instance we were probably lured into making the purchase because of a sale that increased our transactional utility to a level we could not resist; whereas in the second the price just seems unreasonably high, offsetting the significant acquisition utility we would gain from making the purchase.

Finally, we have to make decisions over time about when we close existing accounts and when we open new ones. Known as choice bracketing, this element of the process has interesting effects in its own right (Read *et al.* 1999). Consider the following example proposed by Richard Thaler. You paid for tickets to a sports fixture some months ago, thereby opening a corresponding account when you made the payment and evaluated it according to the acquisition and transaction utilities you received. However, when the day of the fixture arrives, you wake to an unexpected storm that makes the journey to the sports ground exceptionally hazardous. The rational response is for you not to travel and to choose not to attend the match. It is unlikely that you would have purchased the tickets had the weather conditions on the day been forecasted as you would have probably perceived the total cost of the ticket price plus the travel risk to outweigh the utility you would gain. And so it would be irrational for you to take the additional risk on the day. Following the logic of mental accounting, however, you are reluctant to close this account without attending the match because that would immediately translate the cost into a loss, which you would feel keenly and would like to avoid. And so it is likely that you make the journey, hoping to be able to close the account when you return home that evening without any additional cost. This logic also explains why we are likely to sell investments that are increasing in value and to hold on to investments that are making a loss: we are reluctant to close accounts if doing so causes us to experience the feeling of having made a loss, keeping them open for longer than we should and so ultimately making greater losses.

The power of reference points

We cannot physiologically discern the absolute values of temperatures or volumes: we can only judge whether something is hotter/colder or louder/quieter than another. Placing a hand into a bucket of water heated to 20°C, for example, gives us a feeling of warmth if we have previously held our hand in water ten degrees cooler, but a feeling of coldness if we have previously held it in water ten degrees hotter. The bucket of water is the same temperature in both instances but our experience of it is markedly different depending on our reference point. In the same way, we do not evaluate the options from which we choose according to their absolute values. We instead evaluate them against predetermined reference points. A travel company, for example, rationally sells any unsold seats on its bus tour to the Norwegian Fjords at a discounted price: making a smaller profit on each seat is better than making no profit on them at all. A tourist who pays the initial price is not affected by the subsequent discounting but it is likely that he actually enjoys the trip a little less when he discovers the tourist seated next to him paid substantially less. The absolute value of the trip to him has not changed, but his perception of what he should have paid has been reduced, thereby reducing his transactional utility.

We establish our reference points in a variety of ways, depending on the setting. In some cases we base them on our past experiences. Taking advantage of this, two weeks before launching a price promotion for a product – in which its price is to be reduced by 35 per cent – retailers on average raise the price of the product by over 2.5 per cent more than they would do if there was no subsequent promotion (Lan *et al.* 2014). By manipulating upwards the reference price of their customers, retailers can make the subsequent promotion appear more generous than it actually is. In other cases we base our reference points on our own expectations. Coming home to our favourite variety of pizza, for example, is an undeniably positive event even if it is oven cooked. However, the feeling of happiness it causes us is crucially dependent on our expectations. If in the morning we had been told dinner would be salad, the oven-cooked pizza is a very welcome surprise, heightening our happiness. If, on the other hand, we had been told dinner would be delivered by our local pizzeria, the oven-cooked pizza is a grave disappointment, substantially reducing our enjoyment of it. We also base our reference points on the experiences of others, as in the bus tour example above.

Other simplifying heuristics

In addition to the six steps within the editing phase of prospect theory, a whole host of other devices we use to simplify and ease our decision-making has been identified. These are our decision-making heuristics.

One such heuristic is known as the *peak-end rule*. This involves us judging the overall level of pleasure – or displeasure – we feel during an experience based entirely on two pieces of information: the highest level of pleasure during the experience and the level of pleasure at the end. This can substantially reduce the amount of information we process compared to a comprehensive, second-by-second assessment of pleasure levels throughout the experience. Two experiments have been conducted on colonoscopy patients at a hospital in Toronto. In the first experiment, patients were required to report the level of discomfort they felt every 60 seconds during their procedures and to then make judgements afterwards about the overall pain they experienced. The findings showed a 67 per cent correlation between the average of the patients' reported peak and end ratings on the one hand, and their overall pain ratings on the other. In contrast, the correlation between the duration of the procedures and the patients' overall pain ratings was only 3 per cent (Redelmeier & Kahneman 1996). The worst and end levels of pain were more important to patients than the length of their procedures. In the second experiment, patients were separated into two groups and were again required to judge the overall discomfort caused by their procedures. This time, the procedures undergone by one group involved a period of time at the end, lasting for about a minute, when the colonoscope was simply left in place, whereas in the procedures of the other group of patients the colonoscopes were removed as soon as the examinations were complete. The patients were not informed about the experiment. Surprisingly, those in the group subjected to the prolonged examinations reported significantly reduced levels of discomfort overall compared to their counterparts in the normal treatment group. During the period of time when the colonoscope was simply left in place, the level of discomfort felt by a patient was actually reduced and so his *end value* was lower as a result. Despite having longer – and demonstrably more painful – procedures overall, these patients actually reported less overall discomfort (Redelmeier, Katz & Kahneman 2003; Kahneman *et al.* 1997).

We employ the *availability heuristic* to make it easier for us to judge how likely it is that an event will occur. The need for this heuristic arises, once again, because of the difficulty we tend to have with assessing probabilities. The original, and most empirically supported, interpretation is that we judge the likelihood of an event based on how easy it is to think of examples of it occurring (Tversky & Kahneman 1973).[1] For example, and taken from the original work on this, we tend to think the letter "r" appears more frequently in an English dictionary as the first letter of a word than as the third letter in a word, when in reality it is the other way round. This is because we find it easier to think of words beginning with "r" than to think of words in which "r" is the third letter. In a similar way, the fear of swimming in the sea skyrocketed after the release of Peter Benchley's *Jaws* in 1974. An instant success as a novel, rising to the top of best-seller lists where it stayed for almost a year and even selling in landlocked countries such as Tibet – and perhaps even more so in the guise of Steven Speilberg's film of the following year, which was the first to gross $100 million at the box office – the story had a disproportionate effect on our view of sharks. It convinced us that "sharks were a far graver threat to us than they actually are": all because it made it so easy for us to recall images of a shark attack (Eilperin 2013: 48–9). It has also been shown that teachers and lecturers can take advantage of the tendency we have to use the availability heuristic when soliciting ratings of their courses. Asking students to list ten ways in which a course can be improved, rather than just two, results in higher overall ratings of course quality. This is because students find it harder to list ten possible improvements and so, from that, judge the course to be of a higher standard (Fox 2006).

A second simplification rule we employ when judging the likelihood of an event is the *representativeness heuristic* (Kahneman & Tversky 1972). This involves us comparing the event in question to the mental image we have constructed for ourselves of such an event. We then judge the event to be more likely the more closely aligned it is to our mental image, even if that contradicts the conclusions drawn from relevant information. For example:

> *Philip has loved animals since he was a little boy, pressing his parents almost every weekend to take him to the local zoo and establishing something of a pet menagerie at the bottom of their garden. Dolphins and whales have always been his most favourite animals.*
>
> *Which is more likely now that Peter is an adult: he is working as a marine biologist or as a secondary school teacher?*

We are tempted to respond with marine biologist as the answer to this question because Peter's description readily fits our mental image of what a marine biologist would be like whilst growing-up. However, given the numbers of marine biologists and secondary school teachers in the world, the probability of Peter becoming a teacher is orders of magnitude greater than that of him becoming a marine biologist. We ignore much of the relevant information in order to make our judgement easier, basing it on its representativeness. This is a rather trivial example, but such behaviour has much more far-reaching consequences: someone who has kidnapped a child and has then demanded a ransom, for example, is more likely to be convicted than someone who has kidnapped an adult and then has not demanded a ransom (Bernstein 2011). The former case is much more representative of our mental image of a kidnapping.

Decision fatigue

The second half of the explanation for why our consumption behaviour exhibits ranges of price insensitivity and for why we are reluctant to switch utility providers (see Chapter 3) lies in the fact we find decision-making tiring. This is also why we employ so many simplifying steps and heuristics in our decision-making processes, and why we often employ others to make decisions of our behalf, such as personal assistants and secretaries. Psychologists see our acts of volition – such as selecting choices and resisting temptation – as being akin to us going to the gym to lift weights or heading out to plod the streets on a run. The latter involve us physically working out and depleting our energy reserves until we rest and our bodies can replenish themselves. Precisely the same is true of our decision-making, which works and depletes our limited cognitive reserves: known in the literature as our *executive functions* (Baumeister & Tierney 2011). Just as there are limits to the amount of weight we can lift and to the distance we can run at a given moment in time, so there are limits to the number and complexity of decisions we can make: we are cognitively constrained. As our muscles tire from physical exercise, we naturally have to resort to lifting lighter weights and to treading the streets more slowly. In the same way, as we deplete our cognitive reserves through repeated decision-making, three outcomes become increasingly likely:

1. *Our further acts of volition become less effective.* Experiments have been conducted, for example, in which two groups of participants were ushered into separate rooms, where they had to remain for a specified length of time. In one room, the participants were required to solve as many, increasingly complicated problems as they could in the given time. In the other room, in contrast, the participants were able to relax to music and with enjoyable magazines to read. Once the set time had elapsed, both groups were released into a third room in which there was a veritable feast of desirable but unhealthy treats. Controlling for all other possible determinants, the participants in the

problem-solving group consumed significantly more unhealthy food than those in the relaxation group. The act of repeated problem solving tired these participants to such a degree that they did not have sufficient cognitive reserves to resist the temptation as effectively as their more relaxed counterparts (Baumeister *et al.* 1998). A second, and perhaps more troubling, example comes from the behaviour of appeal court judges. Again controlling for all other possible influences, it was found that a prisoner is substantially more likely to be released from custody early if her appeal hearing is at the start of the day rather than at the end. She is also more likely to be successful if her hearing is immediately after the judges' morning break and after lunch than if it is before either recess. The greatest risk for judges comes from releasing a prisoner early who then goes on to reoffend. As they deplete their cognitive reserves during each court session, judges increasingly refuse to offer parole rather than taking this risk when their decisions are increasingly impaired. Taking a break goes someway – albeit to a diminishing extent as the day goes on – to replenishing their cognitive reserves, empowering them to consider more seriously taking that risk (Danziger *et al.* 2011).

2. *We simply avoid further decisions.* When we are required to make a greater number of choices prior to selecting our chosen candidate in an election, for example, the likelihood of us actually abstaining from exercising our democratic right is increased (Augenblick & Nicholson 2009). This is an example of what has become known as the "excessive choice effect": the observation that we actually make fewer choices when faced with an increased number of options. Consider the situation in which we are walking up and down the aisles in a supermarket doing our weekly grocery shop. As we turn into an aisle we notice a display of a variety of different jams and preserves. We are much more likely to look at the jams on display if there is a larger number of them (60 per cent of customers observed in a study of this stopped when 24 jams were displayed compared to 40 per cent when only six jams were displayed). However, we are much less likely to actually make a purchase when faced with a greater range of options (only 3 per cent of the customers faced with the display of 24 jams purchased a jar compared to nearly 30 per cent of those faced with the display of six jams). We have both our interest aroused and our ability to make a

choice reduced by an increased range of options (Iyengar & Lepper 2000).

3. *Cause us to employ more powerful satisficing heuristics.* Perhaps inevitably, businesses take advantage of our constrained abilities to make consumption decisions. Knowing we tire from repeatedly making choices, car manufacturers, for example, order their customization processes such that we encounter the questions with the largest number of possible options at the start. This causes us to cognitively tire earlier in the process, having answered fewer customization questions, than if the questions were randomly ordered. As we tire, we increasingly resort to choosing the default options: the most extreme simplifying heuristic. This enables us to complete the process and to walk away pleased with having customized our new vehicles, but it also increases the amounts we spend and so the profits earned by the manufacturers: without realising it, we are manipulated to choose the options characterized by the largest profit margins (Levav *et al.* 2010).

These are the outcomes of *decision fatigue*: of becoming cognitively tired from decision-making. As we are required to make more numerous or more complex decisions, we deplete our cognitive resources, making it more likely that any further decisions we make will be even more suboptimal, based on heuristics or avoided altogether.

Cognitive load

Psychologists have known for some time that our brains are only able to process limited amounts of information at any given moment: that our working memory capacities are constrained. The *cognitive load* we can process and retain at one time is around seven – plus or minus two – pieces of information (Miller 1956). There are two competing explanations for the causes of this constraint. According to the *slot model*, our working memory consists of a finite number of information "slots" and once they are filled we are simply unable to take in any further information until a slot becomes available. The *spread model*, on the other hand, asserts we continually take in new information but that as we do so we spread our attention evermore thinly across it, to the point at which we cannot recall further information. Recent research suggests there is in fact merit to both explanations, arising from the oscillatory nature of our brain activity. We can only fit a certain amount of information into any given "brain wave", which takes on a higher frequency and so a smaller length when it becomes more important to us; but we have numerous waves operating at any one time, with some dominating others (Miller & Buschman 2015).

The cognitive load we have to bear affects our behaviour in a number of ways (Deck & Jahedi 2015). We tend to be more prone to making reasoning mistakes when we are under an increased cognitive load, for example: our ability to spot flawed logical arguments in syllogisms being inhibited when we have to memorize complex rather than simple dot patterns, for instance (De Neys 2006). We also tend to be more impatient when under cognitive stress: having to memorize a 7-digit, rather than a 2-digit, number for example, makes us 22 per cent more likely to choose chocolate cake over fruit salad when deciding on lunch (Shiv & Fedorikhin 1999). The time it takes us to make moral judgements – such as that about the acceptability of killing a baby in order to save the lives of others – also increases as our cognitive loads increase, although the decisions we reach tend to be unaltered (Greene *et al.* 2008). And we tend to take fewer risks when under a greater cognitive load (Whitney *et al.* 2008). It has also been shown that people of higher cognitive ability – as measured through IQ tests – tend to be more risk-tolerant, more patient and less prone to anchoring effects.

The experience of scarcity impedes the cognitive loads we can bear (Mullainathan & Shafir 2013). When we experience poverty we are less able to attend to important information and so are more prone to making mistakes in our decisions. In one experiment, conducted in a New Jersey shopping mall, subjects were asked to complete IQ tests whilst contemplating one of two financial scenarios. In one scenario, the subject required $150 to repair a car that had broken down. In the other, the subject required $1,500 to cover a range of car-related expenses. The findings revealed that wealthier subjects performed equally well at the IQ tests when contemplating either financial scenario. Poorer subjects, on the other hand, performed much worse in the second scenario than in the first. The experiment was repeated in a real-life situation in India. The subjects in this case were sugarcane farmers, who earn the majority of their income at harvest time each year. The experiment was conducted two months before the harvest, when the farmers were experiencing poverty, and then again two months after the harvest, when the same farmers were experiencing relative prosperity. Confirming the findings of the New Jersey study, the farmers scored on average ten IQ points less in the experiment before the harvest than in the one after (Mani *et al.* 2013).

That scarcity can have significant impacts on our behaviour is shown in a separate experiment conducted on Princeton undergraduates. The students played a game similar to the UK television programme *Family Fortunes* (known as *Family Feud* in the United States), either in time-rich groups having 50 seconds per round or in time-poor groups with only 15 seconds per round. Half the groups, both time-rich and poor, were able to buy more time: one additional second in the current round costing two seconds from their total time endowment for the game. Those in the time-rich groups appeared to actually need less time and rarely chose to buy additional time. Those in time-poor groups who were able to buy additional time chose to do so much more frequently but ended up performing worse overall than their time-poor counterparts who were unable to purchase additional time. This experiment was devised as an analogy for the pay-day loans market: people experiencing poverty are much more likely to borrow money if they can, usually at exorbitant rates of interest, even though doing so reduces their overall financial performance (Shah *et al.* 2012).

Two systems of thinking

A bat and a ball together cost £1.10. The bat costs £1 more than the ball. How much does the ball cost?

Given the advancements we have made in understanding the processes involved in our decision-making, much of which is explored in this chapter, it seems we are characterized by two systems of thinking. We use the first system to make decisions quickly but imprecisely. This involves us reacting to events in an almost automatic fashion, drawing on our gut feelings and intuition. It saves us from becoming cognitively tired and in "fight-or-flight" situations it can prove invaluable in keeping us alive. However, it also leads to us making mistakes. In contrast, we use the second system to make decisions slowly but as accurately as we can. This involves us slowing the decision-making process so we can mentally attend to all the relevant information, deliberating carefully. It enables us to make correct decisions in important situations, but it also tires us cognitively, leading much more quickly to decision fatigue. Both systems are crucial and serve essential functions, but thought needs to be given to which systems we use in which situations. The vast majority of people, for example, respond with 10 pence as the answer to the question above. But if the ball is 10 pence, then the bat is £1.10 and so together they are £1.20. The correct answer is 5 pence. We tend to make this mistake because we subconsciously use our System One thinking to make our decision (Kahneman 2011).

This division of thinking has become evident in the way we make moral judgements: that we do so according to the *Social Intuitionist Model* (Haidt 2001).We make moral judgements on all but the rare occasions when we face particularly difficult and unusual dilemmas through intuition and instinct – through System One thinking. If needed, we then use our System Two thinking to construct reasoned justifications afterwards. Patients who have suffered specific types of brain – prefrontal cortex – damage, for example, retain much of their cognitive reasoning abilities but struggle to make judgements and decisions (see Greene *et al.* 2004; Damasio 2003). And it is rare that we change our judgements through our moral reasoning. This usually only occurs when our reasoning is done socially, through discussion with others, and then we tend to change our judgements for social reasons, such as to bring ourselves in line with social norms (see Chapter 5), rather than through the realization that our initial judgements were wrong.

SUMMARY

- The cognitive capacities we possess are often insufficient to make decisions in a completely optimal fashion: we suffer from *bounded rationality*. As a result, we often *satisfice*, meaning we settle for choices that are good enough.
- Our decision-making is procedural, involving sequences of simplifying steps. This is demonstrated in both *prospect theory* and *mental accounting*.
- We experience different types of utility, such as *acquisition* and *transaction utility*: the welfare we feel from gaining an item for less than the value we assign to it and from the deal itself, respectively.
- We evaluate the options available to us in relation to predetermined *reference points* rather than in absolute terms.

- We employ a variety of simplifying *heuristics* when making decisions, such as the *peak-end rule*, and the *availability* and *representativeness heuristics*.
- We are characterized by *decision fatigue*: we find decision-making cognitively tiring and as we tire we are increasingly likely to avoid further decisions, to resort to default options or to employ increasingly powerful heuristics.
- It is only possible for us to attend to a finite number of pieces of information at any one time: the *cognitive load* we can bear is constrained.
- Our thinking is based on two systems: *System One* thinking, which is intuitive, quick and cheap; and *System Two* thinking, which is deliberative, slow and costly.

Note

1. An alternative interpretation has been proposed in the literature, namely that we judge the likelihood of an event according to the number of cases we can recall of it having occurred (see Schwarz *et al.* 1991).

5

Participation

Mainstream economics has tended to assume that we make our decisions in isolation: that we each selfishly seek to maximize our own utility, unconcerned with the utilities of others (see Chapter 1). That this is demonstrably not the case in many settings is the third facet of behavioural economics and the primary purpose of this chapter.

Goodwill games: the empirical evidence

Belief in the self-interested behaviour hypothesis began to weaken in the 1980s as it was increasingly challenged by findings from a number of games played in conventional laboratory experiments (see Chapter 1). These findings continue to be the bedrock of the empirical evidence that we have wider, more sociable concerns. Six such games are particularly instructive, each predominantly involving only one round and two key players: a *proposer* and a *responder* (the empirical evidence is taken from Fehr & Schmidt 2005; van Winden 2007; Camerer & Fehr 2002).

1. The *Ultimatum Game*: the first, seminal game identifying our social concerns (Güth *et al.* 1982). The game starts with the proposer receiving a set amount of money, the *initial endowment*, which she chooses to distribute, however she likes, between herself and the responder. The responder then either accepts the amount he is offered, triggering the game to end with the money being divided in the manner agreed, or rejects it, causing the game to end with both players walking away with nothing. According to the model of self-interested behaviour, responders should accept any amount offered: even the smallest amount represents an increase in their wealth. Knowing this,

proposers should offer only the smallest amounts, maximizing their gains. The experimental results are very different, however. Offers that represent less than 20 per cent of the initial endowment tend to be rejected by responders 40–60 per cent of the time, with the probability of rejection increasing as the offer becomes less generous. Perhaps in anticipation of this, proposers tend to make offers that represent 40–50 per cent of the initial endowments.

2. The *Dictator Game* (Forsythe *et al.* 1994). This proceeds in the same way as the Ultimatum Game but in this game the responder cannot reject the proposer's offer. Whatever distribution the proposer decides is implemented. In this case, the prediction of the self-interest model is clear – proposers should keep the initial endowments entirely for themselves – but experimental results show they typically divide endowments between themselves and responders 80 per cent to 20 per cent.

3. The *Trust Game* (Berg *et al.* 1995). In this game the proposer is an investor whilst the responder is a trustee, both of whom receive the same initial endowment, E, at the start. The proposer then decides how much of her initial endowment she transfers to the responder, an amount T, knowing that whatever amount she chooses will be tripled. This means the proposer now has an amount E – T and the responder an amount E + 3T. The game ends with the responder deciding how much he transfers back to the proposer, with the players then walking away with the amounts he chooses. Self-interested behaviour would be for responders to transfer nothing at all back to proposers in the final stage. Knowing this, proposers should choose to transfer none of their initial endowments to responders at the outset. And so both players should simply walk away with their initial endowments. Actual results, however, demonstrate that proposers typically transfer about half of their initial endowments to responders, who in turn typically return to proposers the amounts they sacrificed (T). Proposers tend to walk away with E whilst responders tend to walk away with E + 2T.

4. The *Power-to-Take Game* (Bosman & van Winden 2002). This starts with both the proposer and responder again receiving the same initial endowment. The proposer then announces what proportion of the responder's endowment she will seize, after which the responder announces what proportion of his endowment he destroys. The game

ends with the responder walking away with whatever proportion of his initial endowment he has chosen not to destroy, minus the proportion seized by the proposer; and with the proposer walking away with her initial endowment plus the proportion she seizes from the responder's remaining endowment after he has destroyed part of it. The model of self-interested behaviour suggests responders should choose not to destroy any of their endowments if proposers choose to leave them with positive amounts, however small. Therefore, proposers should seize all but the smallest amounts, meaning responders walk away with small but positive amounts and proposers with the maximum amounts they can. Experimental evidence, however, demonstrates that the average seizure rate announced by proposers is around 60 per cent. When proposers announce seizure rates less than 60 per cent, responders choose to destroy on average 8 per cent of their endowments, and when proposer seizure rates are greater than 80 per cent, responders choose to destroy on average 58 per cent of their initial endowments.

5. The *Third Party Punishment Game* (Fehr & Fischbacher 2004). In this three-player game, a judge observes a proposer and responder playing the standard Dictator Game. The game begins with the proposer receiving N tokens and the judge receiving half that number of tokens. The proposer then decides how to distribute her tokens between herself and the responder. Whatever distribution she decides is then implemented. What sets this apart from the Dictator Game is the judge then decides whether or not to punish the proposer for her distribution choice and, if so, how severe that punishment should be. The punishment involves taking tokens away from the proposer, but this is costly for the judge: for every three tokens he takes from the proposer, he loses one token himself. The proposer walks away with her initial endowment of tokens minus both the amount she chooses to give to the responder and the amount taken in punishment. The responder walks away with the amount of tokens he receives from the proposer. And the judge walks away with his initial endowment of tokens minus the cost of the punishment he imposes. Self-interested behaviour would be for the judge to never punish: he receives only cost from punishment. In reality, judges rarely punish proposers if they allocate 50 per cent or more of their initial endowments to

responders, but in approximately 60 per cent of the cases in which proposers assign less than 50 per cent to responders, judges punish them for doing so,with the punishment becoming more severe as the distribution becomes less equal.

6. *Public Goods Games* (see Ledyard 1995). A Public Goods Game involves a group of players, each of whom is given the same initial endowment. Each player has to choose how much of their endowment to contribute to a group project. For each £1 a player contributes, that player and all the others each receives an amount in return from the project that is less than £1, but the group collectively earns a return greater than £1. The group as a whole would benefit most from each player contributing his or her entire endowment, but a self-interested player should personally contribute £0 to the project and to free-ride on the contributions of the others. Experimental results demonstrate that players on average tend to contribute 40–60 per cent of their endowments, although they tend to individually contribute either all or nothing, with approximately a third being purely self-interested. In repeated versions of the game, the amounts contributed by players tend to decline to zero. Public Goods Games with Punishment consist of two stages (Fehr & Gächter 2000). Stage one is precisely the same as above but in Stage 2 all the players' contributions are announced and each player is then able to punish each of the other players. Punishment reduces the punished player's income but, as in the Third Party Game, comes at a cost to the punisher. As such, self-interested behaviour would again entail no punishment being levied, but experimental results show positive amounts of punishment, which in a repeated version of the game tend to lead to contributions increasing round-by-round towards 100 per cent.

Goodwill games: altruism, inequity aversion and reciprocity

Three different types of other-regarding behaviour have been identified in the literature, all of which can be seen in the empirical evidence above:

- *Altruism*, which refers to our desire to see the wellbeing of others increased without us being at all concerned about their behaviour:

it is unconditional kindness and means we are willing to transfer resources to others even if it means making a personal sacrifice.

- *Inequity aversion*, which refers to our desire for the distribution of resources and wellbeing to be equitable across those involved. This has very different implications for the wellbeing of others: if the situation is one in which we possess more than others, we are willing to sacrifice some of what we have to ensure they receive more; but if the converse is true, we seek for resources to be transferred from them to us.
- *Reciprocity*, which drives us to act towards others in the fashion we feel they have acted towards us. We respond kindly to those we perceive have been kind and with hostility to those we perceive have been hostile. This behaviour is determined by our beliefs about the intentions of others.

The results of Dictator Games are suggestive of both altruistic and inequity averse behaviour. There is no reason why proposers should assign any of their initial endowments to responders: there is no recourse available to responders that could harm proposers in any way. That proposers typically choose to give a fifth of their endowments, then, suggests they are concerned either with the wellbeing of their counterparts, or the fairness of the distribution, or both. This interpretation is further supported by the outcomes observed from Ultimatum Games: proposers allocate greater amounts to responders than they would if driven simply by fear of their offers being rejected. Third Party Punishment Games provide further support for inequity aversion, as judges are willing to punish proposers for inequitable choices even at a cost to themselves.

The findings from Ultimatum, Power-to-Take, Trust and Public Goods Games also support the interpretation that we are concerned with reciprocity. This is evident from the behaviour of responders in the first three. When they feel as though they are being treated with kindness – being offered more than 40 per cent of the total and their personal endowments in Ultimatum and Power-to-Take Games, respectively – responders choose to destroy the relevant endowments in only 5 per cent and 8 per cent of cases, respectively. In the case of Trust Games they typically ensure proposers are no worse off as a result of their trust, whilst in Public Goods Games players contribute greater amounts when the others in the group are expected to contribute more and then actually do so.

However, there are clearly limits to our other-regarding concerns. Proposers in both Dictator and Power-to-Take Games seek an 80:20 division of the total endowments in their favour: far from truly equitable outcomes. And responders in Trust Games are not at all concerned about ensuring the gains from proposers' investments are equally shared between them, only about ensuring proposers are no worse off than had they made no investment.

Goodwill games: culture

Our culture – which can be thought of as the social norms to which we have become accustomed – has been found to be an important determinant of our behaviour. One study of the effects of culture ran the Ultimatum Game in fifteen indigenous, small-scale societies across twelve different countries (Henrich *et al.* 2001). Included were four societies that are particularly notable:

The *Machiguenga*. Living in rainforest in Southeast Peru, the 6,000–8,000 Machiguenga people are primarily a community of hunter-gatherers. Families grow crops such as manioc, bananas and sweet potatoes in small gardens, which they supplement with fish, game – such as tapirs, agoutis and peccaries – and other foods they gather from forests and streams. The Machiguenga live and work in small and widely dispersed family groups,which is shown by their lack of personal names: members of the same family group are referred to in terms of kinship, such as mother, father and sister (Shepard, Jr. 1997; Discover Manu 2013).

The *Lamalera*. Living in an Indonesian village on the slopes of a volcanic island in the Indian Ocean, the 2,000 Lamalera people are a traditional whale-hunting society. The *lama fa* – the lead harpooners – lead canoes of twelve or more villagers in hunts, which are so important to the survival of the community that no one who is having any type of trouble at home, or showing signs of any negativity, is allowed to go to sea. The *lama fa* are held in particularly high regard, but everyone involved in a hunt is rewarded with a share of the catch based on their role (Brown 2015).

The *Gnau*. The hill-top villages of the Gnau are found on forested mountain ridges in the West Sepik Province of Papua New Guinea. Each village is sub-divided into hamlets surrounded by coconut palms and has gardens lying in the valleys below. In 1981, the Gnau population was estimated at less than 1,000 people. The people are largely self-sufficient: a family might maintain as many as six gardens, supplementing the crops they grow with food from hunting and gathering. In Gnau society, the giving of a gift establishes an obligation on the part of the recipient to repay with a gift of at least equal value at a time to be determined by the initial giver (*Encyclopedia of World Cultures* 1996a).

The *Aché*. A community of hunter-gatherers, the Aché have lived in eastern Paraguay since at least the 1600s when they met the first Jesuit missionaries. Numbering 614 in a 1987 census, the Aché are divided into four regional groupings. No species are off-limits for the Aché, but the most important game includes peccaries, large rodents, armadillos and coatis. The people walk long distances each day in search of game, with the men hunting in front and the women moving the camps behind. Food is widely shared, with complete and equal sharing of meat. Men have even been observed returning from hunts and explaining they have been unsuccessful, having quietly left their kill at the perimeter of the camp for others to find and share (*Encyclopedia of World Cultures* 1996b).

The results of the Ultimatum Games played by members of these communities are reported in Table 5.1. They show the behaviours experimentally observed in each community are generally consistent with the nature of their everyday lives. The more their lives depend on cooperation and trade, the more their behaviour in the experiments exhibit other-regarding concerns. The Machiguenga and Lamalera peoples, for instance, experience opposite levels of cooperation in their lives. The Machiguenga largely only cooperate in the small-scale production of crops and hunting of game within their restricted and dispersed family units; whereas for the Lamalera the primary form of production is the hazardous hunting of sperm whales, which requires community-wide cooperation. That their experiences of cooperation are so different is revealed in the average offers they make when playing the role of proposers: 26 per cent and 58 per cent, respectively (compared to 40–50 per cent in industrialized countries). The Gnau and Aché peoples, on the other hand, experience opposite levels of trade in their lives. The giving of a gift in Gnau communities represents the establishment of an obligation on the part of the recipient to reciprocate; whereas Aché society is predicated on the sharing of resources, particularly any game that has been hunted. These experiential differences are revealed in the rates at which they reject the offers of proposers when playing as responders: 40 per cent and 0 per cent, respectively.

Table 5.1 Ultimatum Game behaviour in different societies

People	Mean Offer	Rejection Rate
Machiguenga	26%	4.8%
Gnau	38%	40%
Aché	51%	0%
Lamalera	58%	0%

Goodwill games: the players

Games such as those outlined above – perfect examples of conventional laboratory experiments (see Chapter 1) – tend to be carefully designed so the players do not know the identities of one another. This is done to ensure behaviour is not distorted in ways that cannot be observed by the experimenters: such as by feelings of friendship, love or hatred the players bring with them. In cases of repeated games, conducted to investigate the effects of learning, players are usually re-matched at the start of each new round so they continually interact with different people. Such re-matching in Public Goods Games with Punishment causes the contribution levels observed to be lower than when the players are kept in the same groups, but the trend of increasing cooperation round-by-round is unaffected. The trend in the punishments levied round-by-round is also unaffected by re-matching each round, suggesting punishment is not employed to induce players to contribute more to the group in the future but as a reaction to perceived unfairness: it is more a tool of revenge than incentivisation.

Modified Trust Games conducted in real-life scenarios in Germany and the Netherlands have shown the behaviour of undergraduate students to be representative of that in everyday developed-world situations (Fehr *et al.* 2002; Bellemare & Kröger 2004). These experiments also show there are very few individual characteristics that affect such behaviour. The only three that have significant effects are:

- The age of players, with proposers above the age of 60 tending to invest less – and to return more when playing as responders – than their middle-aged equivalents.
- Divorce, with responders who have gone through a divorce within the year leading up to an experiment returning less on average to investors.
- The self-reported health status of the players, with responders who report themselves to be in good health returning more on average to investors.

Goodwill games: other findings

It has been shown – through studies such as that conducted in Indonesia in which participants in an Ultimatum Game could earn the equivalent of three months income – that increasing monetary stakes has little effect on behaviour, only causing a slight reduction in the rejection rates of responders (Cameron 1999). The level of experience of participants has only a limited effect as well. In an Ultimatum Game conducted in Slovakia, for example, the only behaviour in the final round of a series of one-shot games affected by players having greater experience of the game was that of responders, again in the direction of greater reluctance to reject proposers' offers (Slonim & Roth 1997).

It has also been shown that feelings of entitlement and empathy can be important in our behaviour. Two variations of the Power-to-Take Game have been conducted, one in which responders have simply been given their initial endowments, through no effort on their part, and the other in which they have had to earn them. In the subsequent playing of the game, the responders' destruction rates are significantly greater when proposers announce low seizure rates in the first case and significantly greater when proposers announce high seizure rates in the second. The feeling of entitlement generated by earning the money makes us reluctant to impose a cost on ourselves by punishing behaviour we perceive to be relatively fair, but makes us more willing to hurt ourselves when others have treated us unfairly. Two variations of the Third Party Punishment Game have also been conducted. In the first, and most usual, judges have the single role outlined above. In the second, judges are also responders in completely separate Dictator Games. Comparing the outcomes from these two variations, judges punish proposers much more severely in the second case than in the first, bringing punishment levels closer to that observed in situations in which responders choose the punishment themselves. When we can empathize more keenly with others, we act in a way that more closely aligns with what we would want if we were in their situation.

This relates to the nature of the punishment involved. Punishment in Ultimatum Games takes the form of *second-party punishment*: the punishers are those who have been negatively affected by the behaviour of the players to be punished. In Third-Party Punishment Games and Public Goods Games with Punishment, on the other hand, the punishers are not actually harmed by the behaviour of the players to be punished. In these situations – involving *third-party punishment* – the punishment is levied on behalf of other players. Both types of punishment are driven by feelings of unfairness, but second-party punishment tends to be more severe than third-party punishment.

Goodwill games: real life

The six goodwill games explored above all investigate behaviour in artificial and highly controlled experiments, but this certainly does not negate the real-life importance of their results. The dramatic rise of anti-establishment sentiment across both Europe and North America over the past few years – demonstrated most clearly to date in the UK's referendum vote to leave the European Union and the United States's 2016 electoral choice – is arguably the simple manifestation of Ultimatum Game behaviour (see, for example, Beinhocker 2016). The UK is undoubtedly more prosperous now than it would have been had it not joined in 1975 what became the European Union. And both the UK and the United States have benefitted economically from the immigration and trade that has accompanied globalization. In 2016, however, both populations voted to reject these substantial economic benefits, taking the risk of great financial harm. A possible explanation for this lies in their rising feelings of frustration and anger – feelings that were masterfully exploited by Boris Johnson and Nigel Farage in the UK and by Donald Trump in the United States – about the growing inequality and unfairness in their societies, particularly since the 2008 financial crash. The "establishment" in the UK had benefitted from membership of the EU – and in both the UK and the US from immigration and free trade – significantly more than the average person and so the latter rejected their small gains in the name of fairness, just as responders in Ultimatum Games reject offers they deem too small.

Debates surrounding the nature of criminal punishment reflect the behaviour observed in Third-Party Punishment Games. The optimal outcome of any criminal justice system is surely the effective deterrence of crime and the minimization of reoffending rates. However, there have always been people arguing for sentences to be lengthened and incarceration conditions not to be improved: not to increase the deterrent effect but to simply increase the punishment severity out of anger and a desire to see a fairer outcome. Such arguments are being expressed as life-long anonymity for child offenders is being debated in the UK: the main argument in support of such legislation being to maximize the opportunity for young offenders to be rehabilitated into society, and an argument against being the unfairness and indignity such legislation would cause to victims (see, for example, Crook 2014). Punishment is being called for in the name of fairness even at the possible expense of those calling for it.

The smooth functioning of any society is grounded on the maintenance of social norms: of universally accepted and mutually enforced standards of behaviour. That children should be sent to school is a social norm in the UK, as is observing the two-minute silence on Remembrance Day, wearing seat belts whilst driving and casting votes on election days. The vast majority of us adopt these behaviours because we consider them to be the "right things to do". This is precisely the same as the altruistic or reciprocity behaviours we exhibit when playing the games above. We offer 40–50 per cent of our initial endowments when playing as proposers in Dictator Games, we ensure proposers do not lose out when we play as responders in Trust Games and we contribute 40–60 per cent of our endowments to the group project when participating in Public Goods Games because doing so is right. In the food-sharing behaviours of members of small-scale communities in developing countries it has been shown that third-party punishment is crucial for the maintenance of such norms, with the fear of ostracism reinforcing such desirable standards of behaviour (Fehr & Fischbacher 2004).

Emotions

It is suggested that emotions are crucial to understanding the findings from these goodwill games (van Winden 2007). Surveyed about the reasons for their behaviour in Power-to-Take Games, for example, responders consistently report feelings of anger, irritation and contempt. And the strength of these feelings is directly related to the destruction rates they choose: the greater the anger, the greater the proportion of their endowment they destroy. This is also revealed by the different lengths of time it takes responders to make their destruction decisions, shown in Table 5.2 (Reuben & van Winden 2005). Making the decision to destroy either 0 per cent or 100 per cent of their endowments takes responders less than half the time it takes them to choose intermediate destruction rates. Choosing a destruction rate of 0 per cent or 100 per cent is emotionally driven and so emanates from our quick System One thinking (see Chapter 4), whereas choosing an intermediate destruction rate requires slower System Two deliberation.

Table 5.2 Emotions in Power-to-Take Games

Responder's Destruction Rate	Average Decision Time
0%	21.7 seconds
0% < DR < 100%	56.5 seconds
100%	23.0 seconds

It is argued that although perceptions of fairness are important in explaining the behaviour of proposers, they do not appear to be important for the behaviour of responders. In solicited reports about their destruction decisions, there is only a weak link between the choices of responders and their preconceptions of fairness. Their decisions are instead predominantly determined by their emotional reactions to the amounts of money being taken from them. Perhaps these games, then, are not identifying fairness-driven behaviour at all but emotional reactions instead.

There is a growing literature that emphasizes the importance of different types of emotions to our behaviour, beyond the simple angry/happy/sad classification. *Expected emotions* are those we anticipate as a result of taking different actions, whereas *immediate emotions* are those we actually experience at the moment of choosing an action. And the latter consists of *integral* and *incidental emotions*, which are related and unrelated, respectively, to the choice being made (see Rick & Loewenstein 2008). A number of studies have established relationships between our other-regarding behaviour and our emotions by inducing certain feelings in participants who then play variations of the goodwill games above. Two such studies involve undergraduates watching funny or depressing excerpts from films – making them either happy or angry – before playing Public Goods and Gift Exchange Games. Angry players contribute less, punish more severely and overall earn lower amounts than their happy counterparts in Public Goods Games (Drouvelis & Grosskopf 2016). The Gift Exchange Game is a variant of the Trust Game, in which the proposer decides what proportion of his or her initial endowment to transfer to the responder, who then decides how much effort to exert, with greater effort being more costly to the responder but more lucrative for the proposer. Responders in standard Gift Exchange Games exert effort to their own detriment and do so to greater extents when they receive larger transfers from proposers: further evidence of reciprocity. The behaviour of angry responders is no different to this. Happy responders, on the other hand, exert more effort when initial transfers are particularly low but their effort levels do not increase as significantly as transfers become more generous (Kirchsteiger *et al.* 2006). We are more helpful and generous when happy than when angry, showing our moral behaviours crucially depend on our induced, immediate and even incidental, emotions.

Herding

Herding refers to our behaviour when we imitate others in the decisions we make, basing our choices upon the actions of those around us instead of upon our own information. It is popularly held that such behaviour is both irrational and rife in the real world – especially so in financial markets – and is to blame for many of the price bubbles and bursts reported in the news. In reality, however, the evidence for such behaviour is remarkably sparse and inconclusive (see Spyrou 2013). It is also fundamentally difficult to identify herding behaviour because what may appear to be herding may in fact simply be a case of people choosing the same options because they possess the same information and decision-making criteria. And even when herding has been identified, it may be an entirely rational response to the salient incentives acting upon those involved: in the case of an inexperienced investor whose reputation and remuneration depend on not performing less well than the average, for example, it is perfectly sensible for him to "follow the crowd".

Nonetheless having said this, commentators do indeed link herding behaviour to the creation of asset price bubbles: to situations in which the prices of affected assets – shares in technological firms, for example – increase far beyond their actual values as investors scramble to buy them. The US stock market bubble of the late 1990s has been blamed on such behaviour, albeit due to entirely rational behaviour driven by contractual incentives (Dass et al. 2008). The reverse effect – of anti-bubbles – has also been observed, in which asset price bubbles have been destroyed by herd behaviour in the selling of the assets. This has been blamed for the Wall Street Crash of 1929; the US market corrections of 1962 and 1998, of 15 per cent and 19 per cent, respectively; and the Hong Kong crash of 1997 (Welch 2000). It has also been established that financial advisors and analysts are prone to herding in the recommendations they give. From a database of the recommendations of 226 US brokers between 1989 and 1994 it has been shown that analyst recommendations have a positive influence on the subsequent recommendations by fellow analysts (Johansen & Sornette 1999).

Herding behaviour has been observed in non-financial settings. Employers, for example, are prone to being influenced by what they perceive to be the decisions of other employers when short-listing their applicants for interview. In one study, roughly 12,000 fictitious applications were submitted for around 3,000 real job adverts. These applications were designed such that current unemployment spells ranged from 1 to 36 months and all other relevant characteristics were controlled. The association between the length of unemployment and the number of calls to interview was negative: the call-to-interview rate falling from approximately 7 per cent to 4 per cent as the length of unemployment rose from 1 to 8 months, after which it stabilized. Employers at least partially imitate the decisions of other employers; taking the length of unemployment as an indication of the number of rejections a given applicant has already received: entirely rational behaviour in a world in which not all relevant characteristics of an applicant can be observed (Kroft *et al.* 2013).

Herding behaviour has also been observed in an artificial market for music downloads. In a web-based experiment over a 21-week period straddling 2004 and 2005, some 12,200 participants using a music website listened to, rated and downloaded 48 songs. After an initial benchmarking period, the popularity ranking of the songs was inverted so the most popular was listed as having the least popular song's number of previous downloads, the second most popular was listed as having the second least popular song's number of previous downloads, and so on. The songs were listened to over 87,000 times and downloaded over 15,000 times in a pattern demonstrating herding behaviour. A participant was found to be six times more likely to listen to the most popular song (but also three times more likely to listen to the least popular song: an example of *anti-herding*) than to a song in the middle of the ranking. Most songs experienced self-fulfilling prophecies as listeners were influenced by their perceptions of the actions of their fellow listeners. Over time, though, the best songs recovered their popularity (Salganik & Watts 2008).

For whatever reason, then, be it responding sensibly to the information we possess and to the incentives we face, or acting impulsively to our observations of those around us, our behaviour is inherently influenced by the behaviour of others. We are not isolated decision-makers: we are participants in a much wider web of behaviours and influenced by what we see being done by those around us.

SUMMARY

- Most of the evidence of our *other-regarding* preferences has been derived from a small number of experimental games.
- Far from being isolated own-utility maximizers, we exhibit *altruism, inequity aversion* and concerns regarding *reciprocity.*
- *Culture* and *social conditioning* have been demonstrated as important determinants of our sociable behaviour.
- There are few individual characteristics that affect our other-regarding preferences, but feelings of *entitlement* and *empathy* are important.

- Our *emotional responses* are crucial for understanding our sociable preferences, possibly more so than our concerns for fairness.
- Our behaviour is influenced, rationally and irrationally, by the actions we see of those around us: we are prone to herding.

6

Persuasion

Making policy recommendations that seek to manipulate our behaviour by taking advantage of how we actually make decisions is arguably the key distinction between modern behavioural economics and the studies of decision-making that went before it (see Chapter 2). The modern school does not only seek to provide a descriptive theory of behaviour (outlining how we actually behave) – to contrast with and further enhance the normative theory provided by mainstream economics (outlining how in theory we should behave) – it also provides a prescriptive theory of behaviour that outlines how our behaviour can be altered.

Central to this is the approach of *libertarian paternalism*, which involves the government altering the appearance of the choices we face – the *choice architecture* – to guide us towards making the decisions that are best for us. *Libertarian* in that it does not impinge on our freedoms to choose. *Paternalistic* in that it increases our welfare by improving the choices we make. Popularized by the 2008 book of the same name, this is the *nudge* approach to policy-making: nudging us towards better choices. After making every minister in his Cabinet read Thaler and Sunstein's book (2008), former UK Prime Minister David Cameron established the Behavioural Insights Team in 2010 to improve his government's policy-making. Initially a government department, it is now jointly owned by the UK Government Cabinet Office, Nesta and BIT employees, having been part privatized in 2014; it consists of more than 70 employees located in London, New York and Sydney; and it advises authorities around the globe about policy. In 2015, for example, it entered into a three-year partnership with US group Bloomberg Philanthropies on a $42 million project to help local authorities across America use data to engage the public, make government more effective and improve people's lives.

There are various ways in which the choice architecture in a given situation can be altered to manipulate our behaviour: using *decoys*, altering *defaults*, changing the ways in which choices are *framed* and seeking to *prime* or *anchor* us, being just a few. Each of these is examined in this chapter, before moving on to a specific case study and to the arguments that have been levelled against the nudge approach.

The decoy effect

A *decoy* is an option that is demonstrably worse than another in terms of every relevant characteristic (see Huber *et al.* 1982; Simonson & Tversky 1992). As such, we should never choose a decoy if we are presented with one and so it should not affect our decision-making in any way: it should be a completely irrelevant choice. Studies have repeatedly shown, however, that governments can alter our behaviour by introducing such an option into our choice.

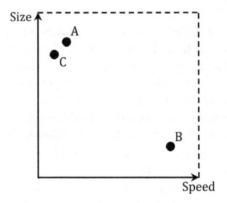

Figure 6.1 The decoy effect

The nature of this effect is illustrated in Figure 6.1, which represents a choice between different cars. Assuming we are only concerned with maximizing the size and speed of the vehicle – price is not a consideration – we tend to split evenly when having to choose between only the two options A and B. When option C is introduced, however, which is a clear decoy because it is asymmetrically dominated in every way by option A, our behaviour changes. We should not consider C for more than a fleetingly small moment, but its presence in the decision draws us towards option A. Those who would have chosen B in the two-option case switch their decision to A, whilst those who would have initially chosen A maintain their decision.

In a recent experimental study of this effect, 95 participants had to choose between shredders X and Y listed below, which are significantly different in terms of both price and the number of pages they can shred at a time. 79.2 per cent of participants chose shredder X whilst 20.8 per cent chose shredder Y.

- Shredder X: priced at $56.95 and able to shred seven sheets at a time.
- Shredder Y: priced at $74.54 and able to shred ten sheets at a time.
- Shredder Z: priced at £102 and able to shred nine sheets at a time.

Shredder Z was then added to the available choices. More expensive and less efficient, this additional option was asymmetrically dominated in every way by shredder Y and so should have been irrelevant to the decisions made. However, in the augmented choice situation, 63.8 per cent of participants chose shredder X and 36.2 per cent chose shredder Y. The addition of shredder Z led to an increase in the demand for shredder Y of 74 per cent (Simonson 2014).

When we face two or more different choices we can find it difficult to evaluate them, especially when they have opposite combinations of desirable characteristics. Introducing a decoy option helps us because it makes the benefits of one of the original options particularly salient. The introduction of shredder Z, for example, makes shredder Y seem to be particularly good, being more efficient and cheaper than the new option. And so we are drawn to the option that dominates the decoy in every way. Magazine companies take advantage of this effect when offering different subscription options. Introducing a digital-only option at the same price as the combined print and digital option, for example, attracts us to purchase the combined option rather than a cheaper, print-only option. Apple also used the decoy effect when it released both its 5C and 5S models in 2013. The 5C, with 32GB memory, was launched for £549. The 16GB 5S, which had considerably more functionality than the 5C, was launched for the same price. The 5C was more expensive than similar models from competing brands and so was never intended to be the option we chose. Its purpose was to make the 5S appear to be much better value for money and so preferable to those of Apple's competitors (Drenth 2015).

The importance of defaults

An early experiment testing the role of default options involved 80 students completing brief questionnaires, each for a payment of $1.50. After doing so, 40 of the participants could exchange their $1.50 for one of two items: a metal pen or a pair of plastic pens. The remaining 40 participants could only exchange their payment for a metal pen. The participants in both cases were told the items available regularly cost more than $2. The result: 75 per cent of participants chose to exchange their payment for the metal pen when it was the only option but only 47 per cent chose to exchange their payment for an item when they could choose either (Tversky & Shafir 1992).

When we are confronted with a clear and tempting alternative, we take advantage of it: we switch our payment for a tangible item of greater value. However, when we have to choose from a number of options, we are inclined to stick with the *default option* and to choose not to act even though doing so is actually beneficial: keeping our $1.50 rather than exchanging it for something more valuable.

The influence of defaults has been investigated – and used to manipulate our behaviour – in an array of settings, such as our energy use, which is becoming evermore important with the rising awareness of climate change (Pichert & Katsikopoulos 2008). One study takes advantage of two natural field experiments in Southern Germany. The first focuses on Schönau, a town of some 2,500 people in the Black Forest. In the 1980s, a local initiative was launched in reaction to the Chernobyl disaster, which eventually led to the electricity supply in Schönau being taken over and switched to an environmentally friendly source in 1997. When the German energy market was liberalized the following year, the environmentally friendly supplier became the incumbent, default supplier. Environmentalism had not been overly significant in the town: the proposal was only just accepted in 1997, the vote being 52 per cent in favour and 48 per cent against, with a turnout of around 90 per cent; and the Green Party only received 5 per cent of the local vote in the 2005 parliamentary elections. In 2006, however, 99.17 per cent of electricity meters in Schönau were still supplied by the more expensive environmentally-friendly supplier, compared to the average proportion purchasing green energy in other German towns being approximately 1 per cent. The second focuses on a separate electricity supplier, *Energiedienst GmbH*, which in 1997 expanded its menu of tariff options. Letters were mailed to 150,000 private and business customers explaining that a hydroelectricity tariff was being made the default, replacing the slightly more expensive single tariff the company had previously offered. Customers wishing to select this tariff did not need to respond. The alternative options outlined in the letter were a fossil fuel powered tariff that was 8 per cent cheaper and a second green tariff that was 23 per cent more expensive. Two months after the letters were mailed, 4.3 per cent of customers had switched to the cheaper tariff, less than 1 per cent had switched to the more expensive green tariff and 0.7 per cent had switched to different suppliers: some 94 per cent remained with the default option.

A related study investigated the effect on our energy use of altering the default setting on our building thermostats (Brown *et al.* 2013). All 93 occupied offices on the first floor of the OECD's Marshall Building in Paris were included in the experiment. The default temperature on the thermostats in the building had usually been maintained at 20°C during the winter months, although occupants had been able to adjust the actual settings, upwards or downwards, by up to 3°C. The experiment consisted of two conditions. In the first condition, the default temperature was reduced by 1°C per week over a three week period. In the second, it was increased by 1°C in the first week (from a starting point of 20°C) and then reduced by 1°C per week for the subsequent two weeks. During the experiment, the occupants in both conditions were observed to adjust the actual thermostat temperatures in exactly the same way, increasing them by the same magnitude irrespective of the default setting, until the default in the first condition hit 17°C at which point the affected occupants increased it by more than those in the second condition. Overall, a 1°C decrease in the default temperature caused a reduction in the average actual thermostat setting of 0.38°C, showing that small reductions in the default temperature settings of building thermostats can lead to lower energy use. If the temperature reduction is too large, however, occupants will over-ride the default effect.

Framing

QUESTION 1: *A rare disease strikes an isolated rural village and the health authority has two possible courses of action. Taking the first will result in 200 of the 600 inhabitants being saved whilst the second gives a one-third probability that all 600 inhabitants will be saved and a two-third probability that none will be saved. Which action do you choose?*

QUESTION 2: *A separate village is subject to periodic natural disasters. The local authority can implement one of two building schemes. The first will result in 400 of the 600 inhabitants dying when the next disaster occurs whereas the second gives a one-third probability that no one will die and a two-third probability that all 600 inhabitants will die. Which scheme do you implement?*

There now exists an abundant, and continually growing, body of evidence that we can be manipulated by the way in which the possible options in a given decision are presented to us. This can be achieved by altering the way in which the options are described, the way in which the information is displayed and the order in which the options are revealed. These are all components in how the decision is *framed*.

It has been demonstrated that framing can be used to take advantage of our inherent loss aversion (see Chapter 3). Responding to the questions above, we tend to choose the first course of medical action in Question 1 because we are repelled by the possibility that none will be saved if we choose the second. When it comes to Question 2, however, we tend to choose the second building scheme because we are attracted by the possibility it offers that no one will die. The options in both questions are actually identical, but we tend to switch our choice because of how they are worded. Those in the first question are expressed in terms of the number of people saved: we take these to be gains and so want to minimize the risk involved. Whereas those in the second are expressed in terms of the corresponding number of deaths: we take these to be losses and so are keen to take the risk to reduce them (Tversky & Kahneman 1981).

One experiment assessed whether or not such loss aversion framing could be fruitfully employed to raise the performance of teachers. 150 teachers in nine schools just 30 miles south of Chicago were randomly separated into two different performance-related-pay groups. Those in the first group were incorporated into a scheme that would pay them each a bonus up to the value of $8,000 at the end of the school year based on the performance of their students. Those in the second group were each given an up-front payment of $4,000 but told that at the end of the year they would either have to return some of it, or would receive up to an additional $4,000, again depending on the performance of their students. The schemes were designed such that teachers in either group would receive the same net bonus if their students performed the same. In the end of year assessments, students whose teachers were in the second group performed significantly better than both those with teachers in the first group and those with teachers in neither group (Fryer *et al.* 2012).

A second experiment, conducted on three groups of nineteen participants at a medical centre in Philadelphia, examined the efficacy of differently framed incentives for people to lose weight over a 16-week period (Volpp *et al.* 2008). Those in the first group – the lottery group – were entered into a lottery with an expected prize of $3 per day if they at least achieved their targeted weight loss. The lottery provided infrequent large payoffs and frequent small payoffs: 1 per cent and 20 per cent chances to earn $100 and $10, respectively. Those in the second group – the investment group – had to invest their own money in the scheme, which they would lose if they failed to achieve their targeted weight loss. At the start of each month, participants in this group were able to invest between $0.01 and $3 per day for the month ahead, which would be refunded in double, plus an additional $3 per day, at the end of the month if they at least achieved their weight loss targets. Those in the third group – the control group – were subject to neither of these incentives. Seventeen of the participants in the investment group made initial investments, averaging $1.56 per day, and fourteen of them held their investments at least constant over the four months of the trial. The results are displayed in Table 6.1. The average 16-week weight loss of those in the control group was 3.9lbs whilst that of those in the lottery group was 13.1lbs and that of those in the investment group was 14lbs. The proportion of those in the control group losing more than 20lbs in total was 5.3 per cent whilst that of those in the lottery group was 26.3 per cent and that of those in the investment group was 36.8 per cent.

In all these studies, expressing the options in terms of avoiding a loss is a significantly more powerful influence on our behaviour than expressing precisely the same options in terms of making a gain.

Table 6.1 The framing of weight-loss incentives

	Control Group	Investment Group	Lottery Group
Total average weight loss after 16 weeks	3.9lbs	14.0lbs	13.1lbs
The average 16-week weight loss range about which we can be 95% confident	0.2olbs - 13.2lbs	9.4lbs - 18.6lbs	7.4lbs - 18.8lbs
Proportion of participants losing more than 2olbs in total	5.3%	36.8%	26.3%
The proportion of participants losing more than 2olbs in total: the range about which we can be 95% confident	0.1% - 26.0%	16.3% - 61.6%	9.2% - 51.2%

A field experiment study of loan advertising in South Africa examined the effects of altering the way in which loan options are *displayed* – rather than *described* – to customers. A single financial provider used a postal campaign to advertise its lending services to 53,194 former clients, all of whom had borrowed money from the firm within the past two years but not within the most recent six months. It did so using a variety of adverts. Some included a person's photograph, others suggestions about how the funds could be used and still others a number of example loans: all information that should be irrelevant to a customer's decision about whether or not to borrow from the firm. The study found that, unsurprisingly, the demand for loans significantly increased as the interest rate charged on loans was reduced. Each 13 per cent reduction in the interest rate increased loan take-up by 4 per cent. Further confirming the excessive choice effect (see Chapter 5), it also found that advertising a single possible loan increases the take-up of loans by 8 per cent compared to advertising four different possibilities. Perhaps most startling, however, was the finding that presenting a photo of a young female adult also increased the take-up of loans, particularly by men, of 8 per cent: the equivalent of reducing the interest rate charged by 26 per cent (Bertrand *et al.* 2010). This suggests we (or is it just men?) are manipulated more effectively by content aimed at triggering us to make intuitive System One responses rather than content that works on our deliberative System Two thinking (see Chapter 5).

The *order* in which options are revealed to us also alters our behaviour. In one laboratory study, for example, 240 students from Hebrew University, aged between 19 and 35 and roughly split evenly across the sexes, were presented with a menu from a local restaurant that consisted of four categories: appetizers, starters, soft drinks and desserts. The participants were randomly assigned across four experimental conditions, each of which was presented with the same menu options but in different orders. No prices were included on any of the four menus. Each participant had to choose one item from each category, motivated by the possibility of being selected in a lottery and winning their chosen meal at the pizzeria from where the dishes had been taken. The overriding result was that all items, irrespective of their popularity, were more frequently chosen when placed either first or last within their category than in the middle (Dayan & Bar-Hillel 2011). To confirm this result in a real-world setting, the researchers approached a small, town-centre coffee shop in Tel Aviv that served approximately 60 items on its menu. The coffee shop agreed to alter its menu such that two different versions were used, each for a period of 15 days, equally distributed across the days of the week. The menus differed in terms of only three categories of items – coffee with alcohol, soft drinks and desserts – from which customers placed 492 orders. Within each category, items at the beginning or the end of the list of choices were chosen approximately 20 per cent more frequently than when they were in the middle of the list: an effect that did not depend on the kind of foods in the category nor on the number of similar items.

Priming

Priming refers to deliberate, but unobtrusive, actions taken by others in one context that alter our mind-sets when making decisions in subsequent contexts without us being aware of their influence. As with the choice architecture alterations explored above, priming is a demonstrably powerful way to manipulate our behaviour, being shown to affect our decisions about the value of options, how much effort to exert on a given task and how to treat others, to name just a few (see Bargh 2006).

Early evidence of priming related to our purchase choices when different types of music were played. Eight wines were specifically displayed in a supermarket: four French and four German, matched pair-wise in terms of their prices and characteristics. The matched pairs were displayed on different shelves, each adorned with the French and German flags; their positions changed halfway through the two-week period of the study. On alternating days, French accordion and German Bierkeller music was played from the top shelf. Across the two weeks there was an overall customer preference for French wine. However, the French wines outsold the German wines particularly strongly when French music was played, whilst the German wines significantly outsold the French alternatives when German music was played (North *et al.* 1997).

A separate example relates to the timing of our expression of honesty. One experiment was conducted on 101 students and employees at US universities. Participants were given two tasks. The first was completing a number of maths puzzles, after which they had to self-declare their rates of success to receive financial rewards. The second was submitting claims for their travel expenses to the laboratory. Some of the participants were required to sign a form confirming the honesty of their two claims at the end of the study; others had to do so at the start, and the remainder not at all. The results are displayed in Table 6.2: the differences between the effects of signing at the end and signing at the start being significant, whereas the differences between the effects of signing at the end and not signing at all being not so (Shu *et al.* 2012). To verify the applicability of these results to scenarios in the real world, a natural field experiment (see Chapter 1) was conducted, involving an automobile insurance company in southeastern United States. Customers of the firm were required to complete policy review forms, which involved them declaring their vehicles' current odometer mileages. Half the customers were required to confirm the honesty of their declarations by signing at the start of the form whilst their counterparts had to do so by signing at the end. The odometer declarations of 13,488 customers, covering 20,741 cars, were examined and the results were clear. The average declared mileage of those who signed at the start of the form was significantly higher than that of those who signed at the end: averages of 26,098 miles and 23,671 miles, respectively. Our behaviour is more honest when we are made to consider our honesty before we act rather than afterwards.

Table 6.2 Priming honesty

	Not signing	Signing at the end	Signing at the start
Proportion of dishonest financial rewards claims	64%	79%	37%
Average travel expense claims	$8.45	$9.62	$5.27

Our behaviour can also be manipulated through *social priming*, both through being primed to be personally more benevolent and through being informed of the benevolence of others. Before playing a Public Goods Game (see Chapter 5), for example, 150 participants in a recent study were split into two groups and tasked with completing a word search as fully as they could in ten minutes. The task consisted of five neutral words (such as "carpet" and "shampoo") and fifteen words associated with cooperation (such as "teamwork" and "collaborative") for one group and twenty neutral words for the other. The participants who were primed to be cooperative went on to free-ride less and to make significantly greater contributions to the group project than the neutrally primed counterparts: average contributions rising from 25 per cent of initial endowments in the latter case to 36 per cent in the former (Drouvelis *et al.* 2015). In this case the priming affected the participants' own preferences about giving but in other studies it has been demonstrated that we tend to donate more to a good cause when told that others have contributed more as well. One study examined the renewal membership contributions of 225 people to a public radio station campaign. Some of the participants were informed that others had recently given more than they had the previous year, whilst some were told that others had recently given less than they had the previous year. The remaining participants were told that others had just matched the contributions they gave the previous year. When the reported contributions of others was lower than a participant's previous contribution, the participant contributed on average $24.05 less than in the previous year; when the reported contributions of others was higher, participants contributed on average $12.08 more than they had in the previous year; and when the reported contributions of others was the same, participants contributed $5.46 more than they had in the previous year (Croson & Shang 2008).

Anchoring

A final way in which our behaviour can be manipulated through alterations to the choice architecture is through *anchoring*. Similar to priming,
anchoring involves deliberately altering our mind-sets as we make decisions, but through making a particular number salient at the start of the
decision-making process rather than drawing our attention to a particular
aspect of the decision in a different context.

The original demonstration of the anchoring effect involved each of a
number of participants first spinning a wheel of fortune consisting of numbers from 0 to 100. Each then had to say whether the number of African
member countries in the United Nations was greater or less than the number identified by their spin, before estimating the actual number of African
member countries in the United Nations. Even though all participants were
fully aware that spinning the wheel was completely unrelated to the correct
answer, their final estimates were significantly related to the numbers their
spins had identified. The participants' estimates were anchored to the numbers they faced beforehand (Tversky & Kahneman 1974).

In a more recent study, the power of anchoring was further demonstrated
in a variety of experimental settings (Ariely *et al.* 2003). In one of these, 55
MBA students at the Massachusetts Institute of Technology were shown six
products, each of which was described but not priced (the average retail
price of the products was $70). The participants were asked to consider
their social security (SS) numbers before being asked whether or not they
would purchase each of the products for a monetary amount equal to the
final two digits of their SS numbers. They were then required to state the
amounts they were actually willing to pay for each of the products, having
been informed that a random device would determine whether they would
have to buy each product at the amount equal to the final two digits of their
SS numbers or at the prices they stated they were willing to pay. The impact
of the SS numbers was significant for every product. Participants with final
two digits of their SS numbers that were above average stated willingness to
pay values between 57 per cent and 107 per cent greater than those whose
final two digits of their SS numbers were below average. In a second experiment, 132 students from the same university were made to listen to a high-
pitched scream lasting 30 seconds. Participants were informed they would
be subjected to another sound, after which some of them would be asked

whether or not they would repeat the exercise if they were paid 10 cents; others were told they would be asked whether or not they would repeat the exercise if they were paid 50 cents; and those remaining were told they would be asked no further question. Participants were also told they would be asked to state precisely how much they would need to be paid to induce them to listen to sounds that differed in duration but were identical in quality and intensity to the one they had just heard. Participants then engaged in a sequence of 9 trials. The results mirrored those from the first experiment: the average amount for which participants would repeat the exercise differed significantly according to the amounts they were initially presented. Those who had been asked whether or not they would repeat the exercise for 50 cents subsequently stated an average price of 59.60 cents, whereas those who had been initially asked whether or not they would repeat the exercise for 10 cents subsequently stated an average price of 39.82 cents. Those who were asked no further question stated an average price of 43.87 cents.

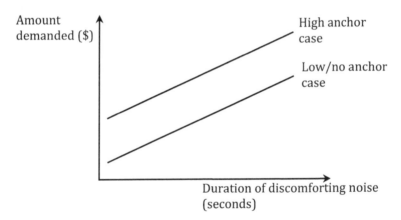

Figure 6.2 Coherent arbitrariness

These final two experiments reveal a further characteristic of our behaviour. We are manipulated by being anchored to different values before making choices, but only in the sense that it shifts our entire preference relations vertically upwards or downwards. The anchor does not affect our valuation of options relative to one another. In the discomforting noise experiment, for example, participants needed to be paid greater amounts to repeat the exercise for noises with greater durations whether or not they were in the low or high anchor groups, but the absolute amounts they demanded differed. This aspect of our behaviour is known as *coherent arbitrariness* because the way we value a range of options is logical but starting from a possibly arbitrary value. It is illustrated in Figure 6.2.

The case of organ donation

The health services of most – if not all – countries face the problem of having insufficient numbers of donated organs to satisfy their demands for transplants. Over 1,300 people either died or became too ill to receive a transplant in the UK whilst being on the national organ transplant waiting list in 2012, and in 2013 there were still over 7,000 people with uncertain futures on that list (NHS Blood and Transplant 2013). Such an immediate and important dilemma has attracted the attention of behavioural economists, particularly regarding the design of organ donation systems.

Countries are divided into two groups. One group of countries have opt-in organ donation registration systems, in which the default is for citizens not to be registered as donors unless they explicitly take action to do so. England is one such country. The other group of countries have opt-out registration systems, in which the default is precisely the opposite: citizens are registered as donors unless they explicitly take action to be withdrawn. A landmark study investigated the effect of changing this default, employing an online experiment to do so. 161 respondents were asked whether or not they were willing to donate their organs if they were to die, some being in an opt-in condition, others in an opt-out condition and those remaining in a condition in which there was no default. Revealed donation rates were approximately twice as high in the opt-out condition as in the opt-in condition, whilst those in the latter condition did not differ significantly from those in which there was no default at all (Johnson & Goldstein 2003). This effect can be seen through the casual observation of effective consent (registration) rates in organ donation systems across countries, such as those in Figure 6.3 in which countries identified with an * have opt-out systems. Countries with opt-out systems also have actual donation rates that are 16.3 per cent greater than those with opt-in systems.

Unfortunately, the issue is considerably more complex than these results portray. Having an opt-out system certainly results in a greater effective

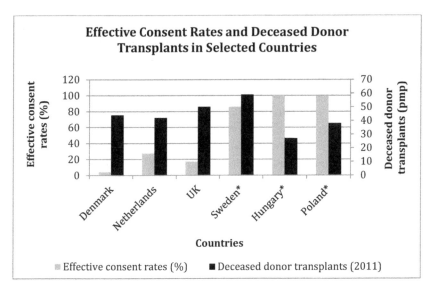

Figure 6.3 The effect of defaults

consent rate but it does not guarantee greater actual donations. Hungary and Poland, for example, both have opt-out systems but, as shown in Figure 6.3, have inferior actual transplant figures than Denmark, the Netherlands and the UK despite their superior effective consent rates (Brennan 2015). In 2012, the UK's Behavioural Insights Team conducted what is possibly the largest randomized control trial to date in order to investigate this issue further. The trial examined a variety of prompts that could be employed to encourage citizens to register with the national organ donation system, having applied for, or renewed, a driving licence on the relevant government website. It investigated the possible effects outlined throughout this chapter. Eight different versions of the prompt were employed over a five-week period, during which time over 135,000 citizens confronted each. All eight variants included the phrase "Please join the NHS Organ Donor Register", but then:

- The *control variant* included no further information.
- The *social cue variant* included the phrase "every day thousands of people who see this page decide to register".
- The *people picture variant* was the same as the social cue version but with an additional picture of a group of people.

- The *logo picture variant* was also the same as the social cue version but with an additional picture of the NHS Blood and Transplant logo.
- The *loss variant* included the phrase "three people die every day because there are not enough organ donors".
- The *gain variant* included the phrase "you could save or transform up to 9 lives as an organ donor".
- The *reciprocity variant* included the phrase "if you needed an organ transplant, would you have one? If so, please help others".
- The *execution variant* included the phrase "if you support organ donation, please turn your support into action".

The results of the trial are displayed in Figure 6.4. The reciprocity variant of the prompt proved to be the most effective alteration to the choice architecture in this situation: 1,203 more people registered under that during the five-week period compared to the control variant. Over the course of a year, this would equate to an increase of 96,000 registrations (Behavioural Insights Team UK 2013).

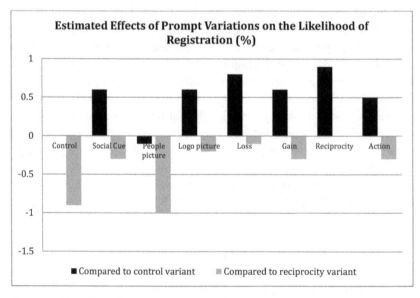

Figure 6.4 The effect of framing

But... the backlash

The many works referenced in this chapter, taken together, demonstrate just how powerful altering the choice architecture can be in manipulating our behaviour in any given situation. This evidence illuminates the tools now available to governments. By introducing decoys, altering defaults, changing the wording or presentation of options, and priming or anchoring us, the government can manipulate us. Doing so to guide us towards choices that are better for us is the central principle of the libertarian paternalism, or nudge, approach to public policy that is now globally widespread. It is certainly not unanimously accepted, however.

The term "libertarian" is for some a misnomer for two distinct reasons. Firstly, true freedom must by definition mean us being able to make, and learn from, our own mistakes. Any intervention by the government to protect us from our own irrationalities is inherently intervention that constricts our freedom. Secondly, altering a situation in such a way that makes it inevitable that we act in a particular manner only affords us the impression – not the experience – of being free. Were Pavlov's dogs really free as they salivated in response to the tolling of a bell?

The term "paternalism" is also a worrying misnomer for some, who question whether any outsider, even a benevolent government, can truly know what is in the best interest of a person. Only when we are in a situation can we determine the course of action that maximizes our welfare and even then it is only the course of action that maximizes *our own* welfare: for a different individual, an alternative course may be more effective. The nudge approach for many also unlocks the door to the possibility of abuse. The assumption hitherto has been that the policy-maker is benevolent, but the tools outlined above can just as easily be employed for the benefit of a self-serving government. The slippery slope argument has been brought to bear on this issue: we may come to regret establishing the social acceptability of libertarian paternalism.

Thirdly, policy-makers are characterized by their own cognitive biases. Some arise from the observation that policy-makers are themselves individuals, subject to loss aversion, decision fatigue and cognitive load constraints like us all. Others arise from group and institutional biases, such as those of herding and groupthink, which lead to collective decisions being suboptimal and even harmful. These, combined with an inevitable lack of necessary information, mean that what can start as well-intended nudging can end as unwelcome, welfare-damaging intervention.

Libertarian paternalists have, of course, responded to these criticisms. We are all subject to nudges every single day. Marketing departments of businesses increasingly strive to manipulate us into giving them our custom, taking advantage of all the tools in this chapter – and more – to part us from increasing amounts of money. In a world in which nudging is a fact of life, the government has an obligation to intervene to offset the malicious nudging of others. Furthermore, and perhaps most convincingly, the studies throughout this chapter reveal the demonstrable benefits such intervention can bring: reducing our energy use, and so climate change; improving the performance of our teachers, and increasing the number of hospital patients saved through transplant operations.

SUMMARY

- *Libertarian paternalism*, also known as the *nudge* approach to policy-making, involves manipulating our behaviour by altering the choice architecture of the decisions we make.
- Introducing a *decoy* – an asymmetrically dominated, and so irrelevant, option – into a decision can attract us to choose the existing option that dominates it entirely.
- We are prone to choosing the *default* option in a given setting and so altering the nature of the default can alter our behaviour.
- *Framing* refers to the way in which available options are described, presented and revealed, all of which can be fruitfully altered to change our decisions.
- *Priming* refers to actions taken in one context that alter our mind-sets when making decisions in subsequent contexts without us being aware of their influence.
- *Anchoring* is the process by which our value relation is shifted vertically by establishing a reference point, maintaining the coherence of our behaviour but around an *arbitrary* point.
- There are many arguments both for and against libertarian paternalism, pertaining to the meaning of freedom, the possibility of paternalism and the biases of policy-makers.

7

Reflections

The emergence of behavioural economics as a field in its own right, over the past 35 years, has fundamentally changed both economics as a subject and the nature of policy-making. Adopting the empiricist approach, behavioural economics has started the process of returning modern economics to the form it took in the eighteenth century. This has not been without critique or contention, however. The purpose of this chapter is to offer a number of reflections – certainly not an exhaustive discussion – about what behavioural economics has already achieved and its future.

Competition, high stakes and experience

Findings have been presented throughout this book that show we do not always behave, or make decisions, in line with the assumptions of rationality generally maintained by economists. A commonly heard retort amongst economists to these findings is that they have been largely generated from laboratory experiments that fail to satisfactorily replicate the real world. When making decisions for real – in situations in which there are significant monetary implications, in which we have substantial experience of such decisions and in which we may actually be in competition with others – these behavioural anomalies will simply dissipate. The high stakes and competition will focus our minds in a way that can never be mirrored in a laboratory and our past experiences will enable us to successfully navigate the pitfalls in a way that we cannot do when faced with experimental questions for the first time (see List 2003, 2004 & 2008).

With the arena of professional sport being one in which participants are highly experienced and in which the competition is fierce to win often substantial monetary rewards, the field of sports economics has come to the fore in examining these doubts. In a study of 239 US Professional Golf Association (PGA) tournaments between 2004 and 2009, encompassing over two and a half million putts by 421 players, it has been shown that professional golfers do indeed exhibit the behaviour predicted by prospect theory (Pope & Schweitzer 2011). The number of shots required for par on a hole is a golfer's reference point and so having to take more shots than that is considered a loss for a golfer. Exhibiting loss aversion – meaning golfers feel the cost of being one over par (a bogey) greater then the gain of being one under par (a birdie) – golfers approach their putts for par with much greater seriousness than their putts for birdie. Golfers also take much more risk when playing putts for birdie than when playing putts for par, confirming another prediction of prospect theory. And the monetary implications of such behaviour are substantial: it is shown that if golfers play their putts for birdie as accurately as they play their putts for par, they would play on average one shot fewer per tournament, which equates to an additional $640,000 in annual earnings for each of the top twenty players.

A similar finding has also been drawn from the behaviour of professional tennis players as they play their first serves at the Wimbledon Championship, one of the four Grand Slam tournaments in professional tennis (Mallard 2016a). Being conditioned to feel losing their service games more acutely than winning them comfortably, the reference point for a tennis player when serving is holding his or her service game. From a dataset of over 2,000 first serves from quarter-final, semi-final and final matches in the men's and women's tournaments from 2010 and 2013, respectively, it has been demonstrated that players are significantly more likely to serve faults when they are ahead in their service games than when they are serving to save them. Players increase their concentration when playing serves to save their service games, desperate to avoid losing them. As in the study above, the monetary stakes in this arena are high: in 2013 the total prize money awarded at the Championship amounted to £22,560,000, with the men's and women's singles champions each receiving £1,600,000.

These findings demonstrate that competition, high stakes and experience do not counteract our behaviours that contradict the standard assumptions of rationality. The findings from the increasing number of field experiments, replicating the perhaps less convincing laboratory experiments, lead to the same conclusion.

Aggregation

A second argument heard from economists to refute the findings of behavioural economics is that the findings will not operate at the level of the market. There are three strands to this reasoning. First, we may all exhibit behavioural anomalies but these will inevitably cancel one another out through our interactions. Second, the inclusion of completely rational individuals in these interactions will serve to highlight the gains that can be made by acting rationally, thereby inducing others to act rationally as well. Third, producers will be incentivised to take advantage of the profitable opportunities that arise to provide services to help us overcome our behavioural weaknesses. At the aggregate level, then, the standard assumptions of rationality represent effectively our average behaviour and the market itself will serve to counteract the behavioural anomalies at the level of us as individuals.

Considering the first of these lines of reasoning, the work of Daniel Kahneman and Amos Tversky, starting with their 1974 paper exploring our biases and heuristics, demonstrates that far from our seemingly irrational behaviours being anomalous, they are in fact common to us all. Loss aversion and its associated traits, for example, have been observed in the behaviour of graduate students, electricity consumers, financial advisors, flood victims, hospital patients and even professional sports people. And in each case it is exhibited in decisions to choose safer-sounding options, to maintain the status quo, to hold onto possessions and to invest more energy and concentration into achieving the reference point outcome than into exceeding it. Working in the same direction, and so being systematic rather than stochastic, the effects of such behavioural traits cannot be cancelled out at the aggregate level. If anything, it is more likely that they are self-reinforced by our interactions.

In thinking about the second and third of these lines of reasoning, consider the example of gym membership. Members of three particular, but certainly not unusual, gyms were offered two packages: they could either pay $70 a month for unlimited usage or buy tickets for ten visits that could be redeemed at any point that year for $100. Across these three gyms, members who were paying monthly were using the facilities on average 4.3 times per month. They were in effect paying $17 per use. These members could clearly have saved money by switching to the alternative package, but for whatever reason chose not to do so (see Della Vigna & Malmendier 2006; Thaler 2016). The important thing is that there was nothing in the market that naturally overcame this seemingly irrational behaviour. There were members on the ten-for-$100 package, but their behaviour did not induce others to follow their lead, and it made no business sense for either these gyms or their competitors to have made consumers aware of their apparent irrationality. Indeed, in many cases such as this – and those of the car dealerships in Chapter 4 and the paper shredder manufacturers in Chapter 6 – it is more profitable for businesses to exploit our behavioural weaknesses than to correct them.

Unnecessary

In 1953, Milton Friedman published his seminal work outlining his view of the nature of economics, which has shaped the subject ever since (Friedman 1953). Friedman claimed the realism of the assumptions upon which economics models are built is irrelevant as long as the predictions of the models are accurate. Economics is to be judged on the efficacy of its predictions rather than on the realism of its arguments. This is the heart of what he termed "positive economics". According to this view, the field of behavioural economics is simply unnecessary. No serious economist has, or ever would, claim we actually make our decisions following the processes outlined by the models of rationality in mainstream economics (see Chapters 1 and 2). Businesses do not actually equate the additional revenue they earn from selling one more unit to the additional cost of doing so when deciding how much of their goods to produce, which is the rule for profit maximization; and we certainly do not construct indifference curves and then choose the consumption bundle that lies on the highest curve we can afford when choosing what we purchase. But that has never been the point. These models were never intended to be lifelike descriptions of behaviour; they were created to make predictions about our aggregate decisions *as if* we behaved in these ways. And they have been remarkably effective in this regard.

The strength of this argument hinges entirely upon what the purpose of economics is taken to be. If its purpose is to make predictions about our behaviour when we are unencumbered by government intervention, then there is certainly merit to Friedman's argument. In this case economists should find the explanations that best fit our revealed behaviour in the simplest way: balancing goodness of fit with parsimony. They should also find the explanations that apply to the widest possible range of situations, maximizing their explanatory power. On both of these fronts, the mainstream models of rational behaviour perform exceptionally well. However, for others the "raison d'être of economics is the application of its principles to the explanation of the malfunctioning of the body politic and economic, and the provision of policies with which to tackle the causes of the malfunctioning" (Harcourt 1994: 460). Policies cannot be introduced to influence our behaviour with any measure of confidence unless our behaviour is truly understood. Two explanations may fit our revealed behaviour equally well, but lead to very different policy implications for how that behaviour should be changed. It is essential to get the assumptions correct and there is no doubt that behavioural economics, by doing precisely this, has made policy-making substantially more effective.

The pension time bomb is a good case in point. It has been long known that developed economies are approaching a crisis. With slowing population growth rates and aging populations, the dependency ratio between those in retirement and those in employment has been steadily increasing, causing state-provided pension schemes to come under increasing strain. The solution is to shift populations away from state to private pensions, but with our inherent inclination to put consumption today ahead of consumption tomorrow (see Chapter 3) we simply do not save enough for our retirement. Following the reasoning of the mainstream economic model of rationality, the solution is clear: governments should subsidize saving for retirement, making it relatively more attractive when compared to current consumption.

In a recent study of the savings behaviour of Danish citizens from 1995 to 2009, the effectiveness of this policy was assessed (Chetty *et al.* 2014). In 1999, the Danish government reduced the tax deduction for saving money in lump-sum pension accounts by the highest earners from 59 cents to 45 cents. The government effectively reduced the subsidy for saving in these pensions and so, according to the prediction of mainstream economics, such saving would be expected to fall as individuals switch to the unchanged annuity pension schemes, to private pension schemes or to current consumption: all of which were made relatively more attractive. And this is precisely what was observed at the aggregate level: average contributions to these lump-sum pension schemes fell by nearly half. However, individual responses were actually very different, with 80.7 per cent of the relevant population making absolutely no change to their savings, continuing to contribute to their lump-sum pensions as before. The aggregate effect was entirely driven by the behaviour of the remaining 19.3 per cent, who stopped contributing to these pensions altogether. And approximately half of the reduction in lump-sum pension contributions was then offset by increased contributions to annuity pension schemes and the rest was almost entirely offset by increased private saving. And so based on this analysis, the reduction in government subsidy had no impact whatsoever on the vast majority of those it affected and, overall, for each $1 reduction in the subsidy, pension saving was reduced by 1 cent.

Standard tools of economic policy in this setting are almost wholly impotent, particularly when compared to the effectiveness of nudging savers to increase their contributions. It is well established that our behaviour is substantially driven by the default options we face (see Chapter 6). By changing the emphasis from us having to deliberately opt-in to pension schemes to being automatically enrolled in them and so having to deliberately opt-out, our participation rates tend to increase from around 20 per cent to 80 per cent (Madrian & Shea 2001). Governments can also increase our overall pension contributions with apparent ease by automatically enrolling us in schemes in which we can select to increase our savings rate in the future in line with increases in our incomes. These automatic escalation – or *Save More Tomorrow* – plans are clever collections of nudges: the automatic enrolment plays on our inclination to stick with default options; having the saving rate increases scheduled for the future plays into our natural present bias; and linking the saving rate increases to our pay rises offsets our loss aversion. In a recent study it has been found that such schemes, in which savings rate increases are not always linked to pay rises, have boosted annual pension savings by $7.4 billion (Thaler & Benartzi 2004 & 2013).

Compassion

Behavioural economics has also made economics, and the policies it recommends, much more compassionate. Since the eighteenth century, philosophers and economic thinkers have assumed we all possess utility functions that translate external events, such as receiving a gift, into a feeling of satisfaction or happiness. For a long time it was believed that it would be possible one day to measure this happiness in a cardinal fashion, just as we do temperature. The units that were to be used were even called *utils*. This belief gradually passed into the background, though, as economists found its realization to be increasingly unlikely. Until recent times, that is. Research in both behavioural economics and neuroeconomics has demonstrated that centres of our brains – or those of primates to be more precise – do indeed act as though they are utility functions. Neurons in these regions fire with increasing intensity as an external event becomes more positive, and the rate at which this happens is even subject to diminishing marginal returns (see Chapter 1). The firing of these pleasure centres in our brains follows the exact logic of the prospect theory utility function displayed in Figure 3.1. This advance opens up the possibility that we will be able to meaningfully compare happiness across people by comparing the intensities of their neural firing, and it means we can examine in much more depth the determinants of happiness for a single person, establishing much more concretely what is meant by rational behaviour for each of us (Park & Zak 2007).

Behavioural economics has established that our happiness also follows the logic of reference point decision-making. We find it difficult to judge how happy we are in absolute terms, instead evaluating our happiness against the level to which we have become accustomed. In the case of happiness, it has also been shown that our reference points adjust over time in response to our experiences. Experiencing a positive event causes us to feel happy, but our feeling of additional happiness is only temporary as our reference points adjust upwards, returning our levels of happiness to our *happiness set points*: akin to the physiological processes of homeostasis within our bodies. This is known as the *hedonic treadmill* as it implies we continually need to experience more positive events in our lives if we are to sustain higher than natural levels of happiness. Recent research has enriched this theory, demonstrating that our happiness set points tend not to be neutral – most of us are positively happy most of the time – and are specific to each of us; that happiness is not a single variable, instead being composed of a range of elements – such as happiness at work and that at home, for example – and so we possess a set point for each component of our happiness; that the rate and extent to which our reference points adjust to our experiences are individual to each of us; and that our natural levels of happiness can change over time (Diener *et al.* 2006).

With such deeper understanding of the nature and determinants of our welfare, it is now possible to design more effective, and also more compassionate, policies. The mainstream model of rational behaviour in economics suggests that unless there are *externalities* – positive or negative effects of our behaviour *on other people* – there is no role for policies to improve welfare. Acting rationally, we already choose the options that maximize our own welfare and so unless by doing so we are inadvertently making the welfare of others less than what it could be, the situation cannot be improved upon. Behavioural economics, however, has clearly demonstrated that in a whole array of situations we do not always choose the optimal options and so there is room for government policies to fruitfully improve our welfare and that of others. This is the heart of the libertarian paternalism – the nudge approach – of Chapter 6.

Behavioural economics has also shown that well-intentioned policies can have harmful, unintended consequences for the very same people they are aimed at helping. The work on cognitive load in Chapter 4, for example, shows that cognitively demanding welfare policies can actually further inhibit those in poverty from making the decisions they need to make to help themselves. If anything, policies are needed to lighten the cognitive load that those in need bear. The implications of the findings above from the study of Danish retirement saving behaviour are also important in this regard. When the Danish government reduced the subsidy to contribute to lump-sum pension schemes in 1999, 80.7 per cent of the affected participants did not respond at all: they simply kept their contributions unaltered. It is highly likely, therefore, that a well-intentioned tax to reduce perceived harmful behaviour, such as that on cigarettes or the widely debated sugar tax, will have an equally impotent effect on consumers. This is most likely to be the case of those in greatest need of help, whose cognitive capacities are particularly constrained because of the draining effects of the scarcity they experience daily. Well-meaning, paternalistic taxes can quickly worsen the situations of those in need: failing to have any effect on consumption and yet exacerbating the scarcity they face. Behavioural economics is invaluable in both identifying these unintended effects and in designing alternative policies to circumvent them.

Weird findings from WEIRD experiments

A striking criticism of the empirical approach employed in behavioural economics is not about its methodology per se, but about the nature of those selected to be its subjects. The vast majority of the experimental findings in the field – as indeed in the fields of experimental psychology and cognitive science as well – have been generated from experiments on WEIRD subjects: on those from Western, Educated, Industrialised, Rich and Democratic societies (Henrich *et al.* 2010).

This arises because, perhaps unsurprisingly, the majority of behavioural experiments are conducted on undergraduate students at the western universities in which behavioural researchers work. It has been shown from a survey of some of the top academic psychology journals between 2003 and 2007, for example, that 96 per cent of experimental subjects were drawn from western industrialised countries. It has also been shown that 67 per cent of the US subjects, and 80 per cent of those from other countries, in the experiments reported in the *Journal of Personality and Social Psychology* were undergraduates (Arnett 2008). The vast majority of subjects studied in behavioural experiments are from the undergraduate population in countries that account for only 12 per cent of the total global population. Although steps are being taken to rectify this imbalance, the typical subject pool in behavioural economics is not substantially more diverse.

This is not necessarily a problem in and of itself. The problem arises as researchers – usually only implicitly – assume their behavioural findings from this remarkably small and rarefied sample reveal universal human traits: that their behaviour is representative of that of the whole global population. The seminal paper on this issue presents a comparison of behaviours of those across: (1) industrialised and small-scale societies; (2) western and non-western societies; (3) US and other western societies, and (4) university-educated Americans and non-university-educated Americans. The findings demonstrate that the subject pool in the majority of behavioural experiments is remarkably narrow and highly unrepresentative of the human race. The behaviour of the majority of participants in behavioural studies is itself an outlier, possibly representing "the worst population on which to base our understanding of *Homo sapiens*" (Henrich *et al.* 2010: 82).

The fundamental weakness?

One recurrent, and for some the most fundamental, criticism of behavioural economics is that it is yet to establish a single, coherent framework through which our behaviour can be studied and understood. According to this view, behavioural economics is essentially a collection of anecdotes about our different behaviours in different situations. It does not offer a plausible alternative to the mainstream model of rationality in economics that can either be taught to undergraduates or employed in economic analysis. And it will always be exposed to the criticism of its approach being arbitrary and ad hoc because there are no guidelines about which type of non-rational behaviour to assume in any given situation: the assumption of one above another will always be seen to be an arbitrary judgement (see Mallard 2016b).

There are three responses to this criticism. The first is one of acceptance: an acknowledgment that it is indeed correct and that behavioural economists should now engage in developing an overarching and unifying theory of our behaviour. As Raj Chetty explained in his 2015 Richard Ely Lecture at the American Economics Association, behavioural economists need to "distil the list of behavioral anomalies into those that are most relevant in common applications", which would "simplify the models under consideration and may ultimately increase the application of behavioral economics" (Chetty 2015: 29). Mainstream economics has had the luxury of time to do this, side-lining, for example, the rare exceptions to the law of demand – the notion that as the price of a product increases, the amount of it we are willing and able to purchase falls – so the fundamental relationship can be established. Behavioural economics, still in its infancy, now needs to engage in the same process.

The second response is that there should be a greater fusion of behavioural and mainstream economics. One such suggestion along this line is the creation of PEEMS: "Portable Extensions of Existing Models" (Rabin 2013). Rather than behavioural economics being developed in such a way that it ultimately replaces mainstream economics, hybrid models should be created, fusing the two. Existing models in economics should be taken as the starting point and then extended to incorporate the findings of behavioural economics whilst keeping the outcome of complete rationality as a special case. A good example of such a model is that of hyperbolic discounting outlined in Chapter 3: the mainstream model of exponential discounting is simply the special case of the hyperbolic discounting model in which the discount rate is constant over time. In this way, models will become both more realistic and also more useful in that they will enable economists to establish the degrees to which actual behaviour mirrors that predicted by the mainstream model in different situations.

The final response is that behavioural and mainstream economics should continue to be developed independently of, and used to complement, one another. The strength of mainstream economics is its ability to construct parsimonious models that explain our behaviour if we were to act with full rationality. Its strength is to establish the optimal case. The strength of behavioural economics, on the other hand, is its ability to expose our actual behaviours in different situations. The two disciplines work in different directions, with different purposes and goals. Their collective strength, then, lies in their distinct specializations and so rather than seeking to either harmonize them or to replace one with the other, the different contributions they can make should be harnessed together. The construction of mainstream models should be continued and used as the starting point for any policy formulation. These policies should then be subject to scrutiny and adjustment in the light of the findings of behavioural economists, which should also be encouraged. Behavioural findings should be used in a way akin to engineering, making predictions and policies more effective (Thaler 2016).

The future

Ever since the eighteenth century and the work of Adam Smith, which essentially launched economics as a subject in its own right, the success of economists has grown beyond measure. Through their increasingly powerful and sophisticated tools of analysis, economists have established a strong understanding of the nature and effects of our economic behaviour, both as isolated individuals and in interactive situations. And through that understanding, they have devised policies to tackle effectively the malfunctioning of the economy: in times of boom and bust, in the terrible situations in which less developed countries find themselves trapped, and in the arenas of environmental degradation, healthcare and political failure, to name just a few. By turning the attention of economists, or at least a proportion of them, back to the empiricist approach favoured by their counterparts in the eighteenth and nineteenth centuries, the field of behavioural economics has without doubt bolstered this success. Developments in behavioural economics have made the subject, and its associated policy toolkit, more effective and more compassionate. It has also made the subject more popular: many more secondary school students are now choosing to pursue the subject at undergraduate level and beyond because of the attraction of behavioural economics and the accessibility of its methodology. Behavioural economics has widened the diversity of the subject and of its students: something that can only be welcomed.

However, there are weaknesses in the discipline, particularly relating to the population base on which its findings are predominantly grounded and to the course that it should navigate in the future. Behavioural economists need to widen the subject sample used in their experiments – across age groups, educational attributes and nationalities – in order to establish traits that are truly common across us all. They also need to increasingly distil the behavioural attributes that are most important and widely applicable to our economic decision-making in order to move the field towards the establishment of a general framework for understanding and analysing our behaviour. This is not so this framework can then replace that of mainstream economics – the two serve different purposes and are both valuable – but so they can be most fruitfully used in conjunction with one another and so behavioural economists can free their field from the criticisms of arbitrariness and ad-hockery that abound.

A final thought. The work on decision fatigue and cognitive load in Chapter 6 has established that we are forever constrained by our mental resources. These are arguably the most important resources we possess and so these constraints are the most critical for our behaviour. Economics is commonly defined as the study of the allocation of our scarce resources across competing demands, but yet the ways in which we allocate our most important resources have not been examined at all. This is potentially the most fruitful path of further research in behavioural economics: to truly understand how we allocate our mental resources across the decisions we make, to understand which decisions we make as optimally as possible and which we content ourselves with satisficing, and to understand how policies can be used to enhance our allocations, to the improvement of our welfare and also that of others. This line of investigation, shifting the focus of study to the higher level of *how we choose* to make our decisions rather than what decisions we make, may even hold the key to the general behavioural theory that is conspicuously absent (see Mallard 2016b).

SUMMARY

- It is argued that competition, high stakes and experience in the real world will abate any behaviour contradictory to the predictions of the mainstream model of rationality in economics. Various studies, particularly of sports economics, have shown this not to be the case.
- It is also argued that such behavioural anomalies will be cancelled out at the aggregate level and by the market mechanism. The systematic nature of our heuristics and biases, and also the self-serving nature of the market, suggest this is not true.
- According to Friedman's construction of *positive economics*, the realism of assumptions, and so the work of behavioural economists, is unimportant. However, the findings of behavioural economists have made government policies much more effective.
- Behavioural economists, by enhancing the understanding of our welfare and widening the toolkit of policy-makers, have made the subject and its policy recommendations much more compassionate.
- The findings of behavioural economists are predominantly drawn from an unrepresentative population sample: from the behaviours of those in western, educated, industrialized, rich and democratic societies.
- For many, the fundamental weakness of behavioural economics is that it is yet to establish a plausible alternative framework for understanding our behaviour to that of mainstream economics. Three responses have been made to this: such a general framework is needed; there should be a greater fusion of behavioural and mainstream economics, and the two disciplines each have their own strengths which should be developed separately.

Glossary

Altruism: behaviour aimed at increasing the wellbeing of others irrespective of their behaviour.

Ambiguity: settings in which the probabilities of the possible outcomes are not known for sure.

Anchoring: a way of altering a person's behaviour by fixing their attention on an initial value.

***As if* assumption**: a view of behaviour designed to represent reality in only an abstract manner.

Aspiration levels: minimum conditions that need to be met for us to be satisfied with an option.

Availability heuristic: judging the likelihood of an event by the ease with which we can think of examples of it occurring.

Bounded rationality: a theory that suggests we are simply unable to make optimal decisions in all but the simplest of settings.

Choice architecture: the way options in a decision setting appear to the decision-maker.

Cognitive load: the amount of information we have to process.

Coherent arbitrariness: valuing a range of options in a logical way but starting from an arbitrary value.

Culture: the social norms to which we have become accustomed.

Decision fatigue: the effect of us becoming mentally tired through decision-making.

Decoy: an option that is demonstrably worse than another in every way.

Default: an option that will be implemented if no other choice is made.

Diminishing marginal utility: consuming further units of a good increases our utility but at a slowing rate.

Empiricism: investigating the world through the gathering and inspection of relevant data.

Endowment effect: our tendency to assign a greater value to an item if we believe it is ours.

Excessive choice effect: our tendency to find decision-making more difficult as the number of options increases.

Experimentation: gathering data about our behaviour in specific and controlled settings.

Framing: the way options are described, presented or revealed.

Herding: behaviour that involves imitation of others.

Heuristic: a rule of thumb we employ to make decision-making easier.

Hyperbolic discounting: reducing the value of future options using a discount rate that declines over time.

Inequity aversion: behaviour aimed at making the distribution of resources more equal.

Inter-temporal decision-making: selecting options for different moments in time.

Libertarian paternalism: government policy that aims to alter behaviour by changing the choice architecture.

Loss aversion: the trait we have of feeling the negative effect of losing something more acutely than the positive effect of gaining it.

Mainstream economics: the generally accepted approach in economics that assumes completely rational behaviour.

Mental accounting: a procedural model of how we choose to spend our limited finances.

Microeconomics: the branch of economics concerned with individual decision-making.

Nudge: another term for libertarian paternalism.

Optimization: identification of the single option that results in the most preferred outcome.

Peak-end rule: a heuristic by which we judge an experience by our feelings at its most extreme and its end.

Preferences: the values we assign to the options available to us when making decisions.

Priming: deliberate, but unobtrusive, actions in one context that alter our mind-sets when making decisions in subsequent contexts.

Procedural model: a step-by-step interpretation of decision-making.

Prospect: a bundle of probabilistic outcomes.

Prospect theory: a procedural model of how we make decisions between prospects.

Rational behaviour: processing all relevant information fully to identify the single utility-maximizing option.

Rationalism: investigating the world through the construction of logical abstract models.

Reciprocity: behaviour that involves being kind to those who have been kind and being hostile towards those who have been hostile.

Reference point: an outcome that we feel as neither a loss nor a gain.

Reflection effect: our tendency to be risk averse when facing a gain but risk seeking when facing a loss.

Representative heuristic: judging the likelihood of an event by how closely it aligns with our mental image of it.

Risk: settings in which the precise outcome is unknown but the probabilities of the possibilities are known with certainty.

Satisficing: identification of an option with which we are satisfied.

Social norms: universally accepted and mutually enforced standards of behaviour.

Status quo bias: our reluctance to move away from the situation in which we find ourselves.

Strategic behaviour: decisions we make that affect, and are affected by, those of others.

System One thinking: decision-making that is quick and intuitive.

System Two thinking: decision-making based on slow and careful deliberation.

Utility: a synonym for wellbeing, welfare and satisfaction.

Utility function: the way outcomes affect our feelings of wellbeing.

References

Ariely, D. 2012. "Real-world endowment", The Blog, www.danariely.com/2012/09/20/real-world-endowment/ (accessed 26 August 2016).

Ariely, D., G. Loewenstein & D. Prelec 2003. "'Coherent arbitrariness': stable demand curves without stable preferences". *Quarterly Journal of Economics* 118, 73–105.

Arnett, J. 2008. "The neglected 95%: why American psychology needs to become less American". *American Psychologist* 63, 602–14.

Arunachalam, B., S. R. Henneberry, J. L. Lusk & F. Bailey Norwood 2009. "An empirical investigation into the excessive-choice effect". *American Journal of Agricultural Economics* 91, 810–25.

Augenblick, N. & S. Nicholson 2009. "Choice fatigue: the effect of making previous choices on decision-making". University of California, Berkeley research paper.

Bargh, J. A. 2006. "What have we been priming all these years? On the development, mechanisms, and ecology of nonconscious social behavior". *European Journal of Social Psychology* 36, 147–68.

Baumeister, R. F. & J. Tierney 2011. *Willpower: Rediscovering Our Greatest Strength.* London: Allen Lane.

Baumeister, R. F., E. Bratslavsky, M. Muraven & D. M. Tice 1998. "Ego depletion: is the active self a limited resource?" *Journal of Personality and Social Psychology* 74, 1252–65.

Behavioural Insights Team UK 2013. "Applying behavioural insights to organ donation: preliminary results from a randomised control trial", https://www.gov.uk/government/uploads/system/uploads/attachment_data/file/267100/Applying_Behavioural_Insights_to_Organ_Donation.pdf. (accessed 24 April 2017).

Beinhocker, E. 2016. "The psychology of voting to leave the EU". *The Atlantic.* http://www.theatlantic.com/politics/archive/2016/06/brexit-voters-self-interest/489350/ (accessed 3 January 2017).

Bellemare, C. & S. Kröger 2004. "On representative social capital". IZA Discussion Paper, Number 1145.

Berg, J., J. Dickhaut & K. McCabe 1995. "Trust, Reciprocity and Social History". *Games and Economic Behavior* 10, 122–42.

Bernstein, D. A. 2011. *Essentials of Psychology*, Fifth Edition. Belmont, CA: Wadsworth Cengage Learning.

Bertrand, M., D. Karlan, S. Mullainathan, E. Shafir & J. Zinman 2010. "What's advertising content worth? Evidence from a consumer credit marketing field experiment". *Quarterly Journal of Economics* 125, 263–306.

Bosman, R. & F. van Winden 2002. "Emotional hazard in a power-to-take-experiment". *Economic Journal* 112, 147–69.

Brennan, S. 2015. "New opt-out system in Wales aims to revolutionise organ donation". *The Guardian*, 25 November. https://www.theguardian.com/society/2015/nov/25/organ-donation-wales-pioneers-opt-out (accessed 3 November 2016).

Brown, T. K. 2015. "Hunting whales with rowing boats and spears". *BBC News Magazine*, 26 April. http://www.bbc.co.uk/news/magazine-32429447 (accessed 1 November 2016).

Brown, Z., N. Johnstone, L. Vong Haščič & F. Barascud 2013. "Testing the effect of defaults on the thermostat settings of OECD employees". *Energy Economics* 39, 128–34.

Bucciol, A., D. Houser & M. Piovesan 2011. "Temptation and productivity: a field experiment with children". *Journal of Economic Behavior and Organization* 78, 126–36.

Burnham, T. C. 2013. "Towards a neo-Darwinian synthesis of neoclassical and behavioral economics". *Journal of Economic Behavior and Organization* 90, S113–27.

Cardenas, J. C. & J. Carpenter 2013. "Risk attitudes and economic well-being in Latin America". *Journal of Development Economics* 103, 52–61.

Camerer, C. & E. Fehr 2002. "Measuring social norms and preferences using experimental games: a guide for social scientists". Institute for Empirical Research in Economics, Working Paper No. 97.

Camerer, C., G. Loewenstein & D. Prelec 2005. "Neuroeconomics: how neuroscience can inform economics". *Journal of Economic Literature* 43, 9–64.

Cameron, L. A. 1999. "Raising the stakes in the ultimatum game: experimental evidence from Indonesia". *Economic Inquiry* 37, 47–59.

Charness, G., U. Gneezy & M. A. Kuhn 2013. "Experimental methods: extra-laboratory experiments – extending the reach of experimental economics". *Journal of Behavior and Organization* 91, 93–100.

Chetty, R. 2015. "Richard T. Ely Lecture: Behavioral economics and public policy: a pragmatic approach". *American Economic Review: Papers and Proceedings* 105, 1–33.

Chetty, R., J. N. Friedman, S. Leth-Peterson, T. Heien Neilsen & T. Olsen 2014. "Active vs. passive decisions and crowd-out in retirement savings accounts: evidence from Denmark". *Quarterly Journal of Economics* 129, 1141–219.

Cornelissen, T., O. Himmler & T. Koenig 2013. "Fairness spillovers – the case of taxation". *Journal of Economic Behavior and Organization* 90, 164–80.

Crook, T. 2014. "Anonymity for serious child criminals is not fair on the accused or the victim". *The Conversation*, 20 May. http://theconversation.com/anonymity-for-serious-child-criminals-is-not-fair-on-the-accused-or-the-victim-26929 (accessed 3 January 2017).

Croson, R. & J. (Y.) Shang 2008. "The impact of downward social information on contribution decisions". *Experimental Economics* 11, 221–33.

D'Exelle, B. & M. van den Berg 2014. "Aid distribution and cooperation in unequal communities". *Review of Income & Wealth* 60, 114–32.

Damasio, A. 2003. *Looking for Spinoza: Joy, Sorrow and the Feeling Brain*. Orlando, FL: Harcourt.

Danziger, S., J. Levav & L. Avnaim-Pesso 2011. "Extraneous factors in judicial decisions". Proceedings of the National Academy of Sciences of the United States of America 108, 6889–92.

Dass, N., M. Massa & R. Patgiri 2008. "Mutual funds and bubbles: the surprising role of contractual incentives". *Review of Financial Studies* 21, 51–99.

Dayan, E. & M. Bar-Hillel 2011. "Nudge to nobesity II: menu positions influence food orders". *Judgment and Decision Making* 6, 333–42.

De Neys, W. 2006. "Dual processing in reasoning: two systems but one reasoner". *Psychological Science* 17, 428–33.

Deck, C. & S. Jahedi 2015. "The effect of cognitive load on economic decision making: a survey and new experiments". *European Economic Review* 78, 97–119.

Della Vigna, S. & U. Malmendier 2006. "Paying not to go to the gym". *American Economic Review* 96, 694–719.

Diener, E., R. E. Lucas & C. N. Scollon 2006. "Beyond the hedonic treadmill: revising the adaptation theory of well-being". *American Psychologist* 61, 305–14.

Discover Manu 2013. "The Machiguenga People". http://discover-manu.org/the-machiguenga-people (accessed 1 November 2016).

Drenth, H. 2015. "The decoy effect". http://www.canicas.nl/en/vision/decoy-effect (accessed 9 November 2016).

Drouvelis, M. & B. Grosskopf 2016. "The effects of induced emotions on pro-social behaviour". *Journal of Public Economics* 134, 1–8.

Drouvelis, M., R. Metcalfe & N. Powdthavee 2015. "Can priming cooperation increase public good contributions?" *Theory and Decision* 79, 479–92.

Earl, P. E. 2005. "Economics and psychology in the twenty-first century". *Cambridge Journal of Economics* 29, 909–26.

Earl, P. E. 2017. "The evolution of behavioural economics". In R. Frantz *et al* (eds) *Routledge Handbook of Behavioral Economics*, 5–17. Abingdon: Routledge.

Eilperin, J. 2013. *Shark: Travels through a Hidden World*. London: Duckworth Overlook.

Ellsberg, D. 1961. "Risk, ambiguity and the savage axioms". *Quarterly Journal of Economics* 75, 643–69.

Encyclopedia of World Cultures 1996a. "Gnau". http://www.encyclopedia.com/ humanities/encyclopedias-almanacs-transcripts-and-maps/gnau (accessed 1 November 2016).

Encyclopedia of World Cultures 1996b. "Ache". http://www.encyclopedia.com/ places/latin-america-and-caribbean/south-american-political-geography/ache (accessed 1 November 2016).

Engle-Warnick, J., J. Escobal & S. Laszlo 2007. "Ambiguity as a predictor of technology choice: experimental evidence from Peru". Working Paper, Cirano.

Fehr, E. & U. Fischbacher 2004. "Third party punishment and social norms". *Evolution and Human Behavior* 25, 63–87.

Fehr, E., U. Fischbacher, B. Rosenbladt, J. Schupp & G. Wagner 2002. "A nation-wide laboratory: examining trust and trustworthiness by integrating behavioral experiments into representative surveys". *Schmollers Jahrbuch* 122, 519–43.

Fehr, E. & S. Gächter 2000. "Cooperation and punishment in public goods experiments". *American Economic Review* 90, 980–94.

Fehr, E. and K. M. Schmidt 2005. "The economics of fairness, reciprocity and altruism – experimental evidence and new theories". Governance and the Efficiency of Economic Systems (GESY), Discussion Paper No. 66.

Forsythe, R. L., J. Horowitz, N. E. Savin & M. Sefton 1994. "Fairness in simple bargaining games". *Games and Economic Behavior* 6, 347–69.

Fox, C. R. 2006. "The availability heuristic in the classroom: how soliciting more criticism can boost your course ratings". *Judgment and Decision Making* 1, 86–90.

Frantz, R. 2004. "The behavioral economics of George Akerlof and Harvey Leibenstein". *Journal of Socio-Economics* 33, 29–44.

Frederick, S., G. Loewenstein & T. O'Donoghue 2002. "Time discounting and time preference: a critical review". *Journal of Economic Literature* 40, 351–401.

Friedman, M. 1953. "The methodology of positive economics". In his *Essays in Positive Economics*, 3–43. Chicago, IL: University of Chicago Press.

Fryer, Jr, R. G. , S. D. Levitt, J. List & S. Sadoff 2012. "Enhancing the efficacy of teacher incentives through loss aversion: a field experiment". National Bureau of Economic Research Working Paper 18237.

Fudenberg, D. & D. K. Levine 2006. "A dual self model of impulse control". Harvard Institute of Economic Research, Working Paper 2112.

Greene, J. D., S. A. Morelli, K. Lowenberg, L. E. Nystrom & J. D. Cohen 2008. "Cognitive load selectively interferes with utilitarian moral judgment". *Cognition* 107, 1144–54.

Greene, J. D., L. E. Nystrom, A. D. Engell, J. M. Darley & J. D. Cohen 2004. "The neural bases of cognitive conflict and control in moral judgment". *Neuron* 44, 389–400.

Güth, W., R. Schmittberger & B. Schwarze 1982. "An experimental analysis of ultimatum bargaining". *Journal of Economic Behavior and Organization* 3, 367–88.

Haidt, J. 2001. "The emotional dog and its rational tail: a social intuitionist approach to moral judgment". *Psychological Review* 108, 814–34.

Haidt, J. 2007. "The new synthesis in moral psychology". *Science* 316, 998–1002.

Harcourt, G. C. 1994. "What Josef Steindl means to my generation". *Review of Political Economy* 6, 460.

Harcourt, G. C. 1995. "Lorie Tarshis, 1911–1993: in appreciation". *Economic Journal* 105, 1244–55.

Harrison, G. W. & J. A. List 2004. "Field experiments". *Journal of Economic Literature* 42, 1009–55.

Hartman, R. S., M. J. Doane & C.-K.Woo 1991. "Consumer rationality and the status quo". *Quarterly Journal of Economics* 106, 141–62.

Heilbroner, R. 2000. *The Worldly Philosophers: The Lives, Times and Ideas of the Great Economic Thinkers.* London: Penguin.

Henrich, J., R. Boyd, S. Bowles, C. Camerer, E. Fehr, H. Gintis & R. McElreath 2001. "In search of homo economicus: behavioral experiments in 15 small-scale societies". *American Economic Review Papers and Proceedings* 91, 73–8.

Henrich, J., S. J. Heine & A. Norenzayan 2010. "The weirdest people in the world?". *Behavioral and Brain Sciences* 33, 61–135.

Hicks, J. R. & R. G. D. Allen 1934. "A reconsideration of the theory of value, part 1". *Economica* 1, 52–76.

Huber, J., J. W. Payne & C. Puto 1982. "Adding asymmetrically dominated alternatives: violations of regularity and the similarity hypothesis". *Journal of Consumer Research* 9, 90–8.

Iyengar, S. S. & M. R. Lepper 2000. "When choice is demotivating: can one desire too much of a good thing?" *Journal of Personality and Social Psychology* 79, 995–1006.

Johansen, A. & D. Sornette 1999. "Financial 'anti-bubbles': log-periodicity in gold and Nikkei collapses". *International Journal of Modern Physics C* 10, 563–75.

Johnson, E. J. & D. Goldstein 2003. "Do defaults save lives?" *Science* 302, 1338–9.

Johnson, E. J. & D. Moggridge (eds) 1987. *The Collected Writings of John Maynard Keynes, Vol 14. The General Theory and After: Part II. Defence and Development.* Cambridge: Cambridge University Press..

Kahneman, D. 2011. *Thinking Fast and Slow.* London: Allen Lane.

Kahneman, D., J. L. Knetsch & R. H. Thaler 1990. "Experimental tests of the endowment effect and the Coase Theorem". *Journal of Political Economy* 98, 1325–48.

Kahneman, D., J. L. Knetsch & R. H. Thaler 1991. "Anomalies: the endowment effect, loss aversion, and status quo bias". *Journal of Economic Perspectives* 5, 193–206.

Kahneman, D. & A. Tversky 1972. "Subjective probability: a judgment of represent-ativeness". *Cognitive Psychology* 3, 430–54.

Kahneman, D. & A. Tversky 1979. "Prospect theory: an analysis of decision under risk". *Econometrica* 47, 263–91.

Kahneman, D., P. P. Wakker & R. Sarin 1997. "Back to Bentham? Explorations of experienced utility". *Quarterly Journal of Economics* 112, 375–406.

Kirby, K. N. & R. J. Herrnstein 1995. "Preference reversals due to myopic discounting of delayed reward". *Psychological Science* 6, 83–9.

Kirchsteiger, G., L. Rigotti & A. Rustichini 2006. "Your morals might be your moods". *Journal of Economic Behavior and Organization* 59, 155–72.

Kroft, K., F. Lange & M. J. Notowidigdo 2013. "Duration dependence and labor market conditions: evidence from a field experiment". *Quarterly Journal of Economics* 128, 1123–67.

Krugman, P. 2009. "How did economists get it so wrong?". *New York Times Magazine*, 2 September, http://www.nytimes.com/2009/09/06/magazine/06Economic-t.html.

Laibson, D., A. Repetto & J. Tobacman 2003. "A debt puzzle". In P. Aghion *et al* (eds), *Knowledge, Information, and Expectations in Modern Economics*, 228–66. Princeton, NJ: Princeton University Press.

Lan, H., T. A. Lloyd & C. W. Morgan 2014. "Supermarket promotions and food prices". Centre for Competition Policy Working Paper, 14-2.

Ledyard, J. O. 1995. "Public goods: a survey of experimental research". In J. H. Roth & A. E. Kagel (eds), *The Handbook of Experimental Economics*, 111–94. Princeton, NJ: Princeton University Press.

Levav, J., M. Heitmann, A. Herrmann & S. S. Iyengar 2010. "Order in product customization decisions: evidence from field experiments". *Journal of Political Economy* 118, 274–300.

Library of Economics and Liberty 2008. "Vernon Smith (1927–)". *The Concise Encyclopedia of Economics*, http://www.econlib.org/library/Enc/bios/SmithV.html (accessed 7 January 2017).

List, J. A. 2003. "Does market experience eliminate market anomalies?" *Quarterly Journal of Economics* 118, 41–71.

List, J. A. 2004. "Neoclassical theory versus prospect theory: evidence from the marketplace". *Econometrica* 72, 615–25.

List, J. A. & S. Levitt 2008. "Homo Economicus Evolves". *Science* 319, 909–10.

List, J. A. & D. Lucking-Reiley 2002. "The effects of seed money and refunds on charitable giving: experimental evidence from a university capital campaign". *Journal of Political Economy* 110, 215–33.

Madrian, B. C. & D. F. Shea 2001. "The power of suggestion: inertia in 401(k) participation and savings behavior". *Quarterly Journal of Economics* 116, 1149–87.

Mallard, G. 2016a. "Loss aversion and decision fatigue at the Wimbledon tennis championship". *International Journal of Behavioural Accounting and Finance* 6, 70–91.

Mallard, G. 2016b. *Bounded Rationality and Behavioural Economics*. Abingdon: Routledge.

Mani, A., S. Mullainathan, E. Shafir & J. Zhao 2013. "Poverty impedes cognitive function". *Science* 341, 976–80.

Miller, G. A. 1956. "The magic number seven plus or minus two: some limits on our capacity to process information". *Psychological Review*, 63.

Miller, E. K. & T. J. Buschman 2015. "Working memory capacity limits on bandwidth of cognition". *Daedalus* 144, 112–22.

Mullainathan, S. & E. Shafir 2013. *Scarcity: Why Having Too Little Means So Much*. New York: Times Books.

Muthukrishnan, A.V., L. Wathieu & A. Jing Xu 2009. "Ambiguity aversion and persistent preference for established brands". *Management Science* 55, 1933–41.

NHS Blood and Transplant 2013. "Taking organ transplantation to 2020: A UK strategy", http://www.nhsbt.nhs.uk/to2020/resources/nhsbt_organ_donor_strategy_summary.pdf. (accessed 24 April 2017).

North, A. C., D. J. Hargreaves & J. McKendrick 1997. "Instore music affects product choice". *Nature* 390, 132.

Okter-Robe, I. & A. M. Podpiera 2013. "Seeing the human face of the global financial crisis", Let's Talk Development: A blog hosted by the World Bank's Chief Economist, 11 April, http://blogs.worldbank.org/developmenttalk/seeing-human-face-global-financial-crisis (accessed on 4 August 2016).

Olsen, R. A. 1997. "Prospect theory as an explanation of risky choice by professional investors: some evidence". *Review of Financial Economics* 6, 225–32.

Page, L., D. A. Savage & B. Torgler 2014. "Variation in risk seeking behaviour following large losses: a natural experiment". *European Economic Review* 71, 121–31.

Park, J. W. & P. J. Zak 2007. "Neuroeconomics studies". *Analyse and Kritik* 29, 47–59.

Pichert, D. & K. V. Katsikopoulos 2008. "Green defaults: information presentation and pro-environmental behaviour". *Journal of Environmental Psychology* 28, 63–73.

Pope, D. G. & M. E. Schweitzer 2011. "Is Tiger Woods loss averse? Persistent bias in the face of experience, competition and high stakes". *American Economic Review* 101, 129–57.

Rabin, M. 2013. "An approach to incorporating psychology into economics". *American Economic Review* 103, 617–22.

Rasiel, E., K. P. Weinfurt & K. A. Schulman 2005. "Can prospect theory explain risk-seeking behavior by terminally ill patients?" *Medical Decision Making* 25, 609–13.

Read, D., G. Loewenstein & M. Rabin 1999. "Choice bracketing". *Journal of Risk and Uncertainty* 19, 171–97.

Redelmeier, D. & D. Kahneman 1996. "Patients' memories of painful medical treatments: real-time and retrospective evaluations of two minimally invasive procedures". *Pain* 66, 3–8.

Redelmeier, D., J. Katz & D. Kahneman 2003. "Memories of colonoscopy: a radomized trial". *Pain* 104, 187–94.

Reuben E. & F. van Winden 2005. "Negative reciprocity and the interaction of emotions and fairness norms". Tinbergen Institute Discussion Paper, TI 2005-014/1.

Ricardo, D. [1820] (1951). "Principles of political economy". Reprinted in P. Sraffa & M. Dobb (eds), *The Works and Correspondence of David Ricardo*, Volume 2; http://oll.libertyfund.org/titles/ricardo-the-works-and-correspondence-of-david-ricardo-vol-2-notes-on-malthus (accessed 24 April 2017).

Rick, S. & G. Loewenstein 2008. "The role of emotion in economic behavior". In M. Lewis, J. M. Haviland-Jones & L. Feldman Barrett (eds), *Handbook of Emotions*, 138–56. New York: Guildford.

Robbins, L. 1932. *An Essay on the Nature and Significance of Economic Science*. London: Macmillan.

Ross, N., P. Santos & T. Capon 2012. "Risk, ambiguity and the adoption of new technologies: experimental evidence from a developing economy". Working Paper, University of Sydney.

Rubinstein, A. 2003 "Economics and psychology? The case of hyperbolic discounting". *International Economic Review* 44, 1207–16.

Rubinstein, A. 2007. "Instinctive and cognitive reasoning: a study of response times". *Economic Journal* 117, 1243–59.

Salganik, M. J. & D. J. Watts 2008. "Leading the herd astray: an experimental study of self-fulfilling prophecies in an artificial cultural market". *Social Psychology Quarterly* 71, 338–55.

Samuelson, P. 1937. "A note on measurement of utility". *Review of Economic Studies* 4, 155–61.

Samuelson, W. & R. Zeckhauser 1988. "Status quo bias in decision making". *Journal of Risk and Uncertainty* 1, 7–59.

Schwarz, N., H. Bless, F. Strack, G. Klumpp, H. Rittenauer-Schatka & A. Simmons 1991. "Ease of retrieval as information: another look at the availability heuristic". *Journal of Personality and Social Psychology* 61, 195–202.

Sent, E.-M. 1997. "Sargent versus Simon: bounded rationality unbound". *Cambridge Journal of Economics* 21, 323–39.

Shackle, G. L. S. 1949. *Expectation in Economics*. Cambridge: Cambridge University Press.

Shah, A., S. Mullainathan & E. Shafir 2012. "Some consequences of having too little". *Science* 338, 682–5.

Shepard Jr., G. 1997. "Native people of the Manu: culture, history and ethnobotany". PBS Online, http://www.pbs.org/edens/manu/native.htm (accessed 1 November 2016).

Shiv, B. & A. Fedorikhin 1999. "Heart and mind in conflict: the interplay of affect and cognition in consumer decision making". *Journal of Consumer Research* 26, 278–92.

Shu, L. L., N. Mazar, F. Gino, D. Ariely & M. H. Bazerman 2012. "Signing at the beginning makes ethics salient and decreases dishonest self-reports in comparison to signing at the end". *Proceedings of the National Academy of Sciences of the United States of America* 109: 15197–200.

Simon, H. A. 1991. *Models of My Life*. New York: Basic Books.

Simonson, I. 2014. "Vices and virtues of misguided replications: the case of asymmetric dominance". *Journal of Marketing Research* 51, 514–9.

Simonson, I. & A. Tversky 1992. "Choice in context: tradeoff contrast and extremeness aversion". *Journal of Marketing Research* 29, 281–95.

Skidelsky, R. 2009. *Keynes: The Return of the Master*. New York: Public Affairs.

Slonim, R. & A. E. Roth 1997. "Financial incentives and learning in ultimatum and market games: an experiment in the Slovak Republic". *Econometrica* 65, 569–96.

Smith, A. [1776] 1982. *An Inquiry into the Nature and Causes of the Wealth of Nations*, Book I 2.2 and Book IV 2.9, http://www.econlib.org/library/Smith/smWN.html (accessed 29 October 2016).

Spyrou, S. 2013. "Herding in financial markets: a review of the literature". *Review of Behavioral Finance* 5, 175–94.

Suri, G., G. Sheppes, C. Schwartz & J. J. Gross 2013. "Patient inertia and the status quo bias: when an inferior option is preferred". *Psychological Science* 24, 1763–9.

Thaler, R. H. 1980. "Toward a positive theory of consumer choice". *Journal of Economic Behavior and Organization* 1, 39–60.

Thaler, R. H. 1981. "Some empirical evidence on dynamic inconsistency". *Economic Letters* 8, 201–7.

Thaler, R. H. 1985. "Mental accounting and consumer choice". *Marketing Science* 27, 15–25.

Thaler, R. H. 1999. "Mental accounting matters". *Journal of Behavioral Decision Making* 12, 183–206.

Thaler, R. H. 2016. "Behavioral economics: past, present and future". *American Economic Review* 106, 1577–600.

Thaler, R. H. & S. Benartzi 2004. "Save more tomorrow: using behavioural economics to increase employee saving". *Journal of Political Economy* 112, S164–87.

Thaler, R. H. & S. Benartzi 2013. "Behavioral economics and retirement savings crisis". *Science* 339, 1152–3.

Thaler, R. H. & H. M. Shefrin 1981. "An economic theory of self-control". *Journal of Political Economy* 89, 392–406.

Thaler, R. H. & C. R. Sunstein 2008. *Nudge: Improving Decisions about Health, Wealth and Happiness*. New York: Penguin.

Trautmann, S. T. & G. van de Kuilen 2015. "Ambiguity attitudes". In G. Keren & G. Wu (eds) *The Wiley Blackwell Handbook of Judgment and Decision Making*, 89–116. Chichester: Wiley.

Tversky, A. & D. Kahneman 1973. "Availability: A heuristic for judging frequency and probability". *Cognitive Psychology* 5, 207–32.

Tversky, A. & D. Kahneman 1974. "Judgment under uncertainty: heuristics and biases". *Science* 185, 1124–31.

Tversky, A. & D. Kahneman 1981. "The framing of decisions and the psychology of choice". *Science* 211, 453–8.

Tversky, A. & D. Kahneman 1992. "Advances in prospect theory: cumulative representation of uncertainty". *Journal of Risk and Uncertainty* 5, 297–323.

Tversky, A. & E. Shafir 1992. "Choice under conflict: the dynamics of deferred decision". *Psychological Science* 3, 358–61.

Uchitelle, L. 2001. "Following the money, but also the mind: some economists call behavior a key". *New York Times*, 11 February.

van Winden, F. 2007. "Affect and fairness in economics". *Social Justice Research* 20, 35–52.

Volpp, K. G., L. K. John, A. B. Troxel, L. Norton, J. Fassbender & G. Loewenstein 2008. "Financial incentive-based approaches for weight loss: a randomized trial". *Journal of the American Medical Association* 300, 2631–7.

Welch, I. 2000. "Herding among security analysts". *Journal of Financial Economics* 58, 369–96.

Whitney, P., C. A. Rinehart & J. M. Hinson 2008. "Framing effects under cognitive load: the role of working memory in risky decisions". *Psychonomic Bulletin & Review* 15, 1179–84.

Index